TEACHING ASSISTANTS' HANDBOOK

A PRACTICAL GUIDE FOR TEACHING ASSISTANTS AND TEACHERS

ROGER SMITH

CREDITS

Author
Roger Smith

Editor
Christine Harvey

Series Designer
Anna Oliwa

Assistant Editor
Jane Gartside

Designer
Erik Ivens

Cover/Illustrations
Edward Eaves

Text © 2004 Roger Smith and Warwickshire LEA
© 2004 Scholastic Ltd

Designed using Adobe InDesign

Published by Scholastic Ltd, Villiers House, Clarendon Avenue,
Leamington Spa, Warwickshire CV32 5PR

www.scholastic.co.uk

Printed by Bell and Bain Ltd, Glasgow

2 3 4 5 6 7 8 9 0   5 6 7 8 9 0 1 2 3

British Library Cataloguing-in-Publication Data
A catalogue record for this book is available from the British Library.

ISBN 0-439-97141-1

CONTENTS

4

INTRODUCTION

6

CHAPTER ONE

WHAT SHOULD TEACHING ASSISTANTS DO?

25

CHAPTER TWO

WORKING IN TEAMS

39

CHAPTER THREE

WORKING WITH CHILDREN WITH
SPECIAL EDUCATIONAL NEEDS

64

CHAPTER FOUR

MANAGING CHILDREN'S BEHAVIOUR AND
BREAKING DOWN BARRIERS TO LEARNING

84

CHAPTER FIVE

TEACHING SKILLS AND CLASSROOM MANAGEMENT

INTRODUCTION

THE CHANGING ROLE OF TEACHING ASSISTANTS

The whole image of teaching assistants in schools is changing. How they are used, what skills they need and what their role is and should be in raising standards has altered radically and irrevocably.

It is no longer the case that teaching assistants can be patronised, as they were only a few years ago, by the phrase 'Mum's army'. The changing expectations of what they do means that they need a whole range of new skills, techniques and strategies. In *The Guardian's* Education supplement (8th May 2001) Laura Barton pointed out that teaching assistants not only work with groups of children and provide physical care, but they also help plan lessons, attend reviews of children with Special Educational Needs and help write reports on them.

In addition, they must all become computer literate, and sometimes learn to communicate through sign language and with children who have different first languages to their own. They must also be familiar with the demands of the National Curriculum and the Literacy and Numeracy Strategies. By developing these skills and reinforcing the professional nature of their role, it will be possible for teachers and schools to use them more effectively in their continuing drive to raise standards and improve educational opportunities.

In October 2000 extra funding became available from the government together with guidance on the use of teaching assistants. *The Guide to Good Practice in the Deployment and Management of Teaching Assistants* (DfES, 2000) suggested that there was a financial commitment to support 20,000 more assistants by 2002. New National Vocational Qualifications (NVQs) covering the work of different levels of teaching assistants, together with courses offered by many other bodies including the Workers' Education Association (WEA) and the Open University all point towards massive development and radical change for the teaching assistant's role.

Many primary schools are already making great strides in workforce reform. The number of teaching assistants in primary schools seems to be growing quickly and a recent government survey in *Excellence and Enjoyment: A Strategy for Primary Schools* (DfES, 2003) suggests that 'the use of support staff has increased in 7 out of 10 primary schools over the last three years. Ninety-seven per cent of headteachers said that the increase had improved teaching and learning' (page 7).

THE CHALLENGE FOR SCHOOLS

The challenge for all schools is to develop the role of teaching assistants in two key areas: to reduce teachers' workload and support better teaching and learning. This challenge, however, has to be seen in the context of where teaching assistants are now in terms of skills, status, pay and career structure. In recognising the growing importance of their role, it is also necessary to balance this out with the recognition that their pay is low and that currently, there are no national conditions of employment or set duties for them. In its simplest terms, what this actually means is that schools are able to be flexible and innovative in what they expect from teaching assistants. At the same time it would be morally wrong not to create a much more generous system of pay, as well as a progressive career structure, that is practical as well as relevant to the needs of both teaching assistants and the school.

The fact is that schools cannot function as effectively as they would like without teaching assistants. We have to relate the new skills and knowledge that teaching assistants need to the effect they can have on raising standards. It is in the interests of all schools to nurture and develop them, because there is an obvious correlation between the better teaching assistant and the success and effectiveness of the school.

ABOUT THE BOOK

This book concentrates on several key areas and, in helping teaching assistants develop their own roles, it will also suggest how schools can contribute to their professional development. There are chapters on the following areas:
● What teaching assistants are able to do and how job descriptions and performance management can develop a professional career structure.
● How teaching assistants can work in a team alongside other professionals and what an effective teaching assistant needs to know.
● The range of support that is needed for children with Special Educational Needs [SEN].
● The skills needed to manage children's behaviour and break down barriers to learning.
● The kind of teaching skills that will help when working with individuals and groups, both small and large, together with how classrooms are managed to maximise learning opportunities.
The chapters contain charts, tables, questionnaires and photocopiable sheets that will be of practical use for individual teachers and teaching assistants, and in training and staff development within the school.

WHAT SHOULD TEACHING ASSISTANTS DO?

WAYS FORWARD IN DEVELOPING TEACHING ASSISTANTS' ROLES

This chapter will attempt to state specifically what teaching assistants should do, and how schools can maximise their impact in the classroom and throughout the school. It also suggests how this can be understood by everyone through job descriptions, as well as examining how teaching assistants' successes and needs can be identified through performance management.

EVALUATING THE IMPACT OF TEACHING ASSISTANTS

In order to think more clearly about what teaching assistants *should* do, it is probably first helpful to think about what they *currently* do and what they are perceived as being good at. The OFSTED report *Teaching Assistants in Primary Schools: An Evaluation of the Quality and Impact of their Work* (OFSTED 2002), raised a number of interesting issues:

● The work of teaching assistants improves the quality of teaching.

● Teaching assistants spend a considerable amount of time supporting teachers in numeracy and literacy. (This is beginning to change the pattern of work for teaching assistants.)

● Training opportunities have helped assistants develop learning support skills.

● Teaching assistants spend less time carrying out more traditional roles, such as photocopying. [This may become a separate and different issue because of the national agreement for tackling teacher workload.]

● Teachers value the input of teaching assistants.

● Managing the work of teaching assistants is recognised as complex and can be difficult – especially when evaluating their impact on children's learning.

● Teaching assistants make valuable contributions to the work of the whole school and have an important pastoral function.

Obviously, OFSTED does not have a monopoly when describing what teaching assistants are good at, and what issues there are surrounding the different roles and expectations that they face. However, OFSTED has summarised successfully the key issues for teaching assistants in their role, which is to:

- improve teaching and learning
- support numeracy and literacy [as well as other areas of learning support]
- contribute to pastoral activities
- help reduce teacher workloads.

CHANGING ROLES

The idea that teachers should take on a more strategic role, and be given more time for lesson planning and preparation, will mean that teaching assistants have to 'take up the slack' and carry out more and more of the routine tasks that have to happen to support teaching and learning. Future changes to the *School Teachers' Pay and Conditions Document* will recognise that teachers should not routinely be required to undertake administrative tasks, including:

- collecting money
- chasing absences
- bulk photocopying
- copy typing
- producing standard letters
- producing class lists
- record keeping and filing
- classroom displays
- analysing attendance figures
- processing exam results
- collating pupil reports
- administering work experience
- administering examinations
- administering teacher cover
- ICT trouble shooting and minor repairs
- commissioning new ICT equipment
- ordering supplies and equipment
- stocktaking
- cataloguing, preparing, issuing and maintaining equipment and materials
- minuting meetings
- co-ordinating and submitting bids
- seeking and giving personnel advice
- managing pupil data
- inputting pupil data.

All the above 'routine' tasks will need to be developed as part of teaching assistants' roles. There have also been suggestions, in the *School Teachers' Pay and Conditions Document (2003)*, that over the next few years cover for short-term absences 'may be provided by persons who are not qualified teachers' (page 174). The document goes on to say that: 'The headteacher will need to ensure that any persons used in this way have been appropriately trained, particularly in pupil behaviour management' (page 174).

Whatever the role that is developed for teaching assistants they will, of course, have to work on such tasks under the strategic supervision of teachers, because handling routine tasks is not the same as having to take professional decisions about them. *Time for Standards: Guidance accompanying the Section 133 Regulations issued under the Education Act 2002* (DfES 2003), makes this extremely clear. It states: 'The support staff member must be subject to the direction and supervision of a qualified teacher in accordance with arrangements made by the headteacher of the school… ' (page 9). Teachers will not lose their control because they will need to make sure that they are still able to be involved in all the routine tasks. In fact, as well as contributing to the success of the routine tasks, teachers will have to make professional decisions about them, analyse their effectiveness, support teaching assistants who are completing them and communicate what needs to be completed to all stakeholders. Routine tasks, after all, are not necessarily trivial tasks, and getting them right will help the school's efficiency and effectiveness.

A cynical question regarding teacher input on routine tasks might be whether this will actually save much time and reduce teachers' workload? Because even if teachers will not be *doing* certain tasks, they will still *arrange how they will be done by someone else* (you, the teaching assistant) and they will still *supervise* how they are completed.

There will need to be an extremely close partnership between teachers and teaching assistants, because many of the proposed tasks will all be part of a shared workload which is set within a proper system of direction and supervision. It cannot be the case that teaching assistants go away somewhere and complete their tasks on their own. If this kind of isolationist role is what is expected to happen, then teaching and learning, and the whole school structure, will be less effective.

TEACHER AND TEACHING ASSISTANT ROLES

Children learn from all adults, each other and the whole, large-scale media bombardment of the 21st century. It is no longer appropriate to categorise teaching assistants as 'non-teaching staff'. As long as schools see themselves as teaching and learning communities it will be more useful to think in terms of everyone being involved in the learning process, and as long as we make sure that there is a clear demarcation of teachers 'directing' the work of teaching assistants, there should be few problems in terms of professional clashes of interest. In other words, teachers should not feel threatened and teaching assistants should not feel put on and used.

To be effective and valued, however, teaching assistants have to be seen to be part of the whole school's efforts to raise standards. There has to be an inclusive teaching and learning culture, where both teachers and teaching assistants are included in the whole school team, in the staff room culture, in lesson planning, and training and development opportunities.

MOVING TOWARDS AN INCLUSIVE TEACHING CULTURE

Some schools will find it easier to work with teaching assistants than others, and there are certain aspects of a school's ethos and culture that will make an inclusive culture easier to implement. Some of the steps towards inclusion and a culture of a shared and effective partnership will mean that the school will be doing most or all of the following:

- Setting priorities within the School Improvement Plan that match teaching assistants to certain specific priorities.
- Using performance management to support the professional needs of teaching assistants, setting appropriate targets for their development and matching their skills to the needs of the children and the school.
- Including teaching assistants in the formal culture of the school, such as planning meetings, decision-making groups, curriculum committees, and so on.
- Including teaching assistants in the informal culture of the school, such as the staff room and social events.
- Communicating with teaching assistants and letting them know what is happening, in terms of daily and weekly messages including times of meetings, for instance.
- Supporting teaching assistants and making them more effective.
- Training teachers to work with teaching assistants effectively.
- Making sure that governors and parents understand how important teaching assistants are in raising standards and supporting teaching and learning.
- Recognising the importance of celebrating achievement and valuing the amount of work that is done by teaching assistants.
- Recognising that teaching assistants can provide:
  - additional teaching and learning support for children,
  - more effective teaching and learning for specific children with special educational needs (SENs),
  - a more consistent approach to behaviour management,
  - emotional support to teachers,
  - local information and knowledge about the community.

CREATING AN EFFECTIVE TEACHER–ASSISTANT PARTNERSHIP

An effective partnership between teachers and assistants can be simplified by seeing it as creating a shared balance within how the curriculum is planned and taught. There are a number of key roles in this partnership.

SHARING THE PLANNING OF THE CURRICULUM
Teachers and teaching assistants will need time to discuss and share planning outside teaching time.

SHARING THE PREPARATION FOR THE LESSON
This will include sharing the preparation of resources and materials, as well as any necessary photocopying, and so on. Teaching assistants will also need time to help prepare resources and set up the classroom.

TEACHING THE LESSON
Teaching assistants will have a key role to play in this. Not only will they need to know what they have to do, but in working with individuals and groups they will need to use skills that involve encouraging, instructing, questioning, repeating, assessing, recording, interpreting, challenging, praising, reprimanding, and so on.

REVIEWING AND EVALUATING THE LESSON

It is important that teaching assistants are able to bring new ideas to teaching and learning and what is happening in the classroom, as well as contributing to any lesson evaluation. They will be able to share reflections on how the children have worked, and whether the objectives of the lesson were met.

THE IMPORTANCE OF JOB DESCRIPTIONS

So far we have looked at what teaching assistants do in relatively general terms. But this will be difficult to do in schools unless it is possible to move from the general acceptance of what their work is, to specific descriptions of what it is they actually do on a day-to-day basis. Teaching assistants need to know what their role is, and teachers need to be able to measure the successful work of a teaching assistant against agreed criteria. This is especially important in performance management where, in most effective schemes, the job description will form the starting point of any discussion. Job descriptions will become even more important when there are different grades of teaching assistant and where there is movement up pay spines. It is difficult to envisage how this movement will work unless it is based on measurable success against the agreed criteria within a job description.

DRAWING UP A JOB DESCRIPTION

The first important general point to make when drawing up a job description for a teaching assistant, is that there needs to be a balance between the following:
● supporting the curriculum
● supporting the learning
● supporting the teacher
● supporting the school.

This balance in the above areas will reflect that teaching assistants are there to support learning directly, for example within the Literacy Hour. They should also carry out what can be seen as very routine tasks, such as putting up displays or photocopying, which will help teachers manage their own workload so that they are able to focus on their core tasks.

IDENTIFYING LEVELS OF WORKLOAD

One way of understanding the different kinds of support that teaching assistants can offer is to see their job in terms of different levels. Historically, there are some very good reasons for being a teaching assistant, especially in terms of hours of work and being at home during the school holidays. However, generous pay and opportunities for career development have not traditionally been provided as strong incentives, and primary schools have mainly used one level or grade of teaching assistant with little or no opportunity for any formal career progression. This lack of a career structure is changing and unions such as UNISON, which represents many teaching assistants, is developing structures in which teaching assistants can work on several levels.

GRADING TEACHING ASSISTANT SKILLS

Since the workload remodelling agreement for teachers, many LEAs are also beginning to resolve issues of career structure for teaching assistants, and one of the most common structures that is being developed is based on three grades. These grades are a prelude to an improved salary structure and are also a way forward in taking decisions about the relationship between teachers and teaching assistants. In particular, as part of the recent workload agreement, the grades may be a deciding factor in whether teaching assistants will be able to teach groups of children. For example, it may become the case that teaching assistants who are on a version of Grade 3 will be teaching groups if and when required and dependent on the training that is needed. Both LEAs and schools will be creating guidelines that they find suitable. The following grades are based loosely on recent information collected from Warwickshire LEA.

TEACHING ASSISTANT GRADE 1

Teaching assistants at Grade 1 will receive direction and be accountable to the class teacher, but will also be expected to exercise some initiative and independent action. They would be expected to carry out basic tasks, such as organising and tidying equipment, record keeping, keeping children safe during activities such as PE and providing support for learning activities in the classroom (see the specific list of Teaching Assistant Grade 1 Skills Criteria, photocopiable page 17).

TEACHING ASSISTANT GRADE 2

Teaching Assistants at Grade 2 will work under the direction of the class teacher, but will also be accountable to the special educational needs co-ordinator (SENCo) where this is appropriate. They will be expected to exercise initiative and independent action, and provide specialist support in areas such as SEN, literacy or numeracy.

All these responsibilities will be in addition to those expected of a teaching assistant at Grade 1 (see the specific list of Teaching Assistant Grade 2 Skills Criteria, photocopiable page 18).

TEACHING ASSISTANT GRADE 3

It is possible that some larger schools, or those with a very significant number of children on the SEN register, will introduce a third grade of teaching assistant. This will be a senior position and a Grade 3 assistant will work under the direction of the SENCo without the need for close supervision. Teaching assistants on this grade will have greater curriculum knowledge, and more skills and specialist knowledge, for developing the learning of children with special educational needs. There are now also Higher Level Teaching Assistants (HLTAs) who are able to take whole classes, under the direction and supervision of a teacher, as well as plan their own roles in lessons. In addition to the criteria expected of teaching assistants at Grades 1 and 2 (see the lists of Teaching Assistant Grades 1 and 2 Skills Criteria, photocopiable pages 17 and 18), Grade 3 teaching assistants will need to demonstrate that, after appropriate training, they can:

- Supervise and act as line manager to Grade 1 and 2 teaching assistants.
- Cover a teacher's classes for short periods of absence under the overall direction of another teacher.
- Use teaching and behaviour management skills to take more control of supporting SEN children outside the direct supervision of the SENCo.

Examples of tasks that Grade 3 teaching assistants will undertake, include contributing to lesson planning, assessing children's learning and recording it, helping children develop specific skills, leading small scale developments, liasing with parents, and supporting and even managing other teaching assistants.

The kinds of levels that are described overleaf, and which will be able to be used in formulating job descriptions, will be useful because they will help to:

- provide incentives
- give recognition to specific tasks
- recruit competent and effective people
- differentiate between different types of work
- begin to produce a differentiated pay structure which rises incrementally.

USING SKILLS LISTS TO CREATE JOB DESCRIPTIONS

When schools and LEAs create specific lists of the skills necessary for the different grades of teaching assistant it will become possible to create precise job descriptions for each grade. The example overleaf shows the kind of job description that will be suitable for a teaching assistant who is working at Grade 2.

Job Description
Teaching Assistant

Name _____

Post _____

REPORTING LINES
● The teaching assistant is ultimately responsible to the headteacher under the general supervision of a class teacher and assistant headteacher.
● When working with some children, the SENCo may undertake the overall supervisory responsibility.
● On a day-to-day basis the teaching assistant will work under the direction of the class teacher.

TASKS
Tasks allocated to the teaching assistant:
● Working under the direction of the class teacher to promote the intellectual, social and emotional development of the children in accordance with the aims of the school.
● Assisting class teachers in planning and working with children.
● Working with both individuals and groups of children, as appropriate, under the class teacher's direction.
● Assisting teaching staff in the general supervision and welfare of children on the school premises, during school hours and at times of arrival and dispersal.
● Assisting teaching staff in the general supervision and welfare of children on visits away from school.
● Looking after classroom equipment and equipment in other designated areas.
● Helping in the preparation and clearing up of teaching areas.
● Assisting teachers in assessing and recording children's achievements.
● Assisting teachers in their administrative tasks.
● Helping teachers create an appropriate learning environment by displaying children's work and other materials.

SKILLS DEVELOPMENT
It is also possible to use the graded skills criteria lists for teaching assistants to help recognise many essential areas for their development. The most important of which will include skills that are necessary:
● for working with individuals and groups
● for supporting behaviour issues
● for working alongside children at different levels of SEN
● to work in teams with other colleagues and teachers.
    All these key areas will be explored in later chapters. At this stage it is

important to reinforce the complexity of the teaching assistant's role and to remind us how crucial the link is between different grades and appropriate job descriptions (job descriptions that are precise enough to be meaningful but also simple enough to be understood). Both the grade summary and the job description have to be able to be used in ways that can form the backbone of an effective performance management strategy.

Here is a checklist of areas to develop before and during the process:

● Teachers need to understand their role in managing another adult in the classroom and may well need some training.

● Teaching assistants who spend most of their time working alongside children in developing their learning have to have an impact. There need to be straightforward strategies to monitor and evaluate the effect the teaching assistant has on individuals and groups. This may be as simple as evaluating test scores before and after the teaching assistant's input.

● Each teaching assistant must know which teacher they are working with. If they work in different classes it is important that one person, perhaps the deputy head, SENCo or assistant head, has an overview of their work.

● Teaching assistants work best when supporting specific children or small groups of children within curriculum areas, such as literacy or numeracy. It is important that they know what the overall objectives are and what the objectives for their particular child or group of children are.

● Teaching assistants need to feel that they are part of the whole school and that they have a place in the wider picture of school life. It is important to try and include them in training opportunities and regular meetings.

PERFORMANCE MANAGEMENT

By using the criteria within the different grades of teaching assistants, the specific roles within the job description, the broad skills needed and those areas of the job that need developing, it is possible to create an effective performance management process that helps the school and you, the individual teaching assistant. It is essential to make performance management the core of school improvement because it is where targets are set that are directly related to raising standards. It is equally important to make sure that teaching assistants are part of it. It is a cyclical process with five basic stages:

1. Observation

5. Training needs set

2. Performance review meeting

4. Targets set

3. Review of last year's targets and job description

If teaching assistants are to be seen as valued professional colleagues then it is important for headteachers, deputies, assistant heads and class teachers to take responsibility for supporting them in their professional development. In fact the DfES document *Time for Standards* (2003), suggests that: 'a key responsibility of the headteacher will be to ensure that the support staff member has the skills, experience and expertise required to carry out the "specified work"... ' (page 10). Performance management plays a key part in this responsibility. It will help teaching assistants raise levels of achievement by:

- recognising what they have achieved and what they intend to achieve
- helping them to recognise existing skills and improve their performance
- improving the quality of the work that they do
- recognising, identifying and improving their strengths and potential
- identifying appropriate training needs.

If the system of performance management that they become part of is effective and non-threatening, most teaching assistants will learn from their successes and failures and begin to identify their own strengths and weaknesses. This process of self-evaluation should play a principle role in the development of teaching assistants. This is especially true of performance management, because it involves making judgements about professional competence.

GATHERING INFORMATION

One of the best ways to approach performance management is to see it as a way of gathering as much information as possible so that it can be shared with you, the teaching assistant, and then used to move everyone forward by making them more effective. Doing this will benefit the school and help raise standards.

The first stage in the performance management cycle is for your 'team leader', who can be your class teacher, the deputy head or even the headteacher, to observe you working. This should not be seen as a casual occasion and there needs to be a simple pro forma, such as the 'Observation form' on photocopiable page 21. During the observation, the team leader gathers as much information as possible to help them complete the 'Observation form'. It is this information that is used as part of the discussion in the performance review meeting.

THE PURPOSE OF THE PERFORMANCE REVIEW MEETING

The performance review meeting is at the core of the performance management process. It is a review of your achievements in the past year measured against previous targets, and a look towards the future and setting new targets.

The meeting should not be in any way one sided. It should not be a situation in which a teacher or senior school manager is telling you, the teaching assistant, what to do. It should be a sharing of ideas, so that mutually acceptable targets are set for the coming year. It will be a better meeting if you are given a copy of your current job description so that you can compare what it says with the realities of your job before the meeting. If it is available, a summary of the key priorities in the School Improvement Plan [SIP] for the current year would also improve the effectiveness of the meeting.

SELF-APPRAISAL QUESTIONNAIRE

The meeting will also be more effective if you consider what your successes have been beforehand. Prior to the meeting you need an opportunity for an honest self-review that should reduce the chances of any major surprises during the review meeting.

The 'Self-appraisal questionnaire' (photocopiable pages 19–20) can be used for this and is closely linked to the skills criteria outlined in the teaching assistant grades (photocopiable pages 17–18).

HOLDING THE REVIEW MEETING

The review meeting shouldn't last more than 45 minutes, as a fixed time will help concentrate the mind. It is at this meeting that ideas are shared about the tasks that have been completed during the year, and future targets and training needs are identified and agreed. There are three further forms to be completed. This may sound like a bureaucratic nightmare, but it isn't. The forms are simple and short and they are important, because they will be used in the following year's review meeting and for measuring your work against specific targets. This is so that you can move through and up the appropriate pay spines that are related to your status as Grade 1, 2 or, although this will not be the norm in mainstream schools, Grade 3.

The 'Review meeting summary' (photocopiable page 22), the 'Target setting form' (photocopiable page 23) and the 'Training and development needs' form (photocopiable page 24) should be completed as far as possible during the review meeting and agreed, through discussion, by you and your team leader. The team leader needs to take the forms away to make sure that they are a true record before a copy is finally given back to you. This is because they will form the basis of your work as a teaching assistant during the coming year, be used during any mid-year monitoring of targets, as well as forming the starting point for the next cycle of performance management.

CONCLUSION

This chapter has summarised the changing role of teaching assistants, as well as the diverse nature of the work they will be doing in the classroom and in the whole school context. The job has to have much more structure than perhaps it ever had in the past, and both specific job descriptions and performance management will help create this structure, as well as beginning to formalise teaching assistants' roles and recognising their continuing importance.

Each teaching assistant has a key role to play in raising standards and improving the effectiveness of teaching and learning. Despite the diverse nature of the role, and the continuing importance of undertaking tasks that will help teachers reduce their workload, the most important part of teaching assistants' work will continue to be with children in the classroom. It is because of this that teaching assistants need to be increasingly knowledgeable, flexible and innovative in how they approach their work alongside teachers.

TEACHING ASSISTANT GRADE 1 SKILLS CRITERIA

SUPPORTING THE CURRICULUM
- Support children's learning as directed by the teacher.
- Foster independence and self-esteem with children identified by the teacher.
- Facilitate discussions with groups of children.
- Encourage children to discuss and reflect on their work and achievements.

SUPPORTING CHILDREN
- Provide appropriate levels of support as identified by the teacher, including promoting increased attention, helping children stay on task, helping with physical difficulties, encouraging independence.
- Extend play-based learning with younger children.
- Reinforce behaviour strategies with children who are working towards behaviour targets.
- Work alongside the teacher and other adults in supervising children in school and on outside visits.
- Provide comfort and care to distressed children and care for children with minor cuts and grazes.
- Have an understanding of SEN as defined in the SEN Code of Practice.

SUPPORTING TEACHERS
- Prepare resources.
- Contribute to class displays.
- Prepare practical areas and be prepared to leave rooms clean and tidy.
- Assist the teacher in their record keeping processes by providing relevant information and completing appropriate assessment sheets.
- Provide feedback to the teacher about learning activities.
- Assist the teacher in the management of classroom behaviour.
- Undertake routine administrative tasks, such as preparing resources and photocopying.

SUPPORTING THE SCHOOL
- Understand the roles and responsibilities of this level of teaching assistant.
- Participate in appropriate induction training and performance management processes.
- Maintain confidentiality according to the school's and legal requirements.
- Maintain school policies, and health and safety regulations.
- Attend staff meetings where appropriate and relevant.
- Understand the roles and responsibilities of all other adults in the school.

PERSON SPECIFICATION
EXPERIENCE
- Demonstrate an ability to understand and work within the SEN Code of Practice.
- Have experience of working with children of the appropriate age.
- Have experience of ICT as a tool for improving learning.

SKILLS
- Relate well to both children and adults.
- Have good communication skills.
- Persuade and negotiate with both children and adults.
- Have good listening skills.
- Work successfully in a team.
- Be directed by teachers and take the initiative when required.

PERSONAL QUALITIES
- Have natural authority.
- Be sensitive to the needs of children.
- Be flexible and adaptable.
- Be committed to own professional development.
- Show willingness to undertake appropriate training.
- Be trustworthy and discreet.
- Offer clear behaviour boundaries.
- Have a good sense of humour.

Based on material © Warwickshire LEA

TEACHING ASSISTANT GRADE 2 SKILLS CRITERIA

All the criteria for Teaching Assistant Grade 1 together with the following:

SUPPORTING THE CURRICULUM
- Contribute to planning the curriculum in the short-term.
- Work alongside the teacher in introducing lessons.
- Interact with the teacher and children as agreed and as is appropriate.

SUPPORTING THE CHILDREN
- Begin to be aware of the kind of support necessary for both individuals and groups without teacher assistance.
- Support children in groups outside the classroom.
- Begin to develop own behaviour strategies.

SUPPORTING THE TEACHER
- Monitor individual and group achievement of each lesson's key objectives and give feedback to the teacher.
- Be actively involved in the management of the classroom, including taking responsibility for care and preparation of resources.
- Help in the assessment of children by observation as well as working through tests.
- Record information that is relevant to the assessment and review of children's progress.
- Attend Individual Education Plan (IEP) and other meetings related to SEN.
- Support and maintain the implementation behaviour strategies.
- Undertake appropriate administrative tasks.

SUPPORTING THE SCHOOL
- Have an up-to-date knowledge and working understanding of the SEN Code of Practice.
- Understand the school's policies that deal with behaviour, SEN, numeracy and literacy.
- Liase with parents, carers and share information that is relevant to individual children.

PERSON SPECIFICATION
EXPERIENCE
- Have experience of teaching assistant work.
- Be working towards NVQ level 3, or have equivalent knowledge, experience and skills.

SKILLS
- Have a very good level of knowledge and understanding of at least one area of learning, such as literacy, numeracy, SEN, early years.
- Present relevant information to other adults working in school.
- Be able to and want to acquire new skills.
- Be able to and want to take some responsibility for planning own work.
- Exercise initiative.
- Take independent action.

PERSONAL QUALITIES
- Be able to act independently of the teacher and to use initiative when appropriate.

Based on material © Warwickshire LEA

SELF-APPRAISAL QUESTIONNAIRE

Read each statement carefully and tick the appropriate response.

1 means that you consider yourself good at this.

2 means that you are OK but need to improve and develop this area of your job.

3 means that this an area you consider yourself weak in.

It is logical to expect that your performance management targets are more likely to be based, and in fact should be based, on those responses that you tick as **2** and **3**.

GENERAL AREAS	1	2	3
A I help and encourage children to respect each other.	☐	☐	☐
B I help children to respect each other's property.	☐	☐	☐
C I help children to accept responsibility.	☐	☐	☐
D I encourage children to take responsibility.	☐	☐	☐
E I help develop high quality relationships.	☐	☐	☐

WORKING WITH TEACHERS IN THE CLASSROOM	1	2	3
A I influence children's behaviour in the classroom.	☐	☐	☐
B I help teachers with their lesson planning.	☐	☐	☐
C I cater for the learning needs of all the children I work with.	☐	☐	☐
D I use a wide range of resources.	☐	☐	☐
E I work with individual children.	☐	☐	☐
F I work with allocated groups of children.	☐	☐	☐
G I attend staff development courses and other training.	☐	☐	☐

HELPING WITH THE CURRICULUM	1	2	3
A I read the teacher's plans.	☐	☐	☐
B I understand the content of the lessons I support.	☐	☐	☐
C I am able to adapt the lessons to fit the needs of the children I support.	☐	☐	☐
D I am able to help with assessment.	☐	☐	☐
E I help each teacher complete his or her curriculum planning sheets.	☐	☐	☐

WORKING WITH SPECIAL EDUCATIONAL NEEDS [SEN] CHILDREN	1	2	3
A I support a range of children with SEN.	☐	☐	☐
B I know what individual children's SEN are.	☐	☐	☐
C I know which children are on the SEN register.	☐	☐	☐
D I am aware which children are gifted and talented.	☐	☐	☐
E I help teachers complete Individual Education Plans [IEPs].	☐	☐	☐

CONTINUED...

SELF-APPRAISAL QUESTIONNAIRE – CONTINUED

UNDERSTANDING WHOLE SCHOOL ISSUES

	1	2	3
A I understand which areas of the curriculum the teachers I work with are responsible for.	☐	☐	☐
B I understand and have discussed my job description with an appropriate teacher and/or my performance management line manager.	☐	☐	☐
C I understand the communication processes in the school.	☐	☐	☐
D I know what my responsibilities are related to supervision at break times and lunchtimes.	☐	☐	☐
E I understand and take part in the school's performance management system.	☐	☐	☐
F I am aware of the school's consistent methods of planning and assessment.	☐	☐	☐
G I have read the current school development plan.	☐	☐	☐
F I have a copy of the current school prospectus.	☐	☐	☐

TRAINING AND DEVELOPMENT NEEDS

	1	2	3
A I already have some relevant qualifications.	☐	☐	☐
B My performance management review recognised some relevant training needs.	☐	☐	☐

	1	2	3
C I am aware of the training opportunities for teaching assistants.	☐	☐	☐
D I regularly take advantage of training opportunities.	☐	☐	☐
E I have already had some literacy training.	☐	☐	☐
F I have already had some numeracy training.	☐	☐	☐
G I have attended in-school training on training days	☐	☐	☐

RELEVANT PERSONAL QUALITIES

	1	2	3
A I am able to relate to children and discuss both their work and their personal problems with them.	☐	☐	☐
B I am able to discuss teaching and learning strategies with teachers, and try to resolve any problems in a professional way.	☐	☐	☐
C I work well in a team that includes both teachers and teaching assistants.	☐	☐	☐
D I am able to offer professional support to children.	☐	☐	☐
E I am able to offer professional support to colleagues.	☐	☐	☐
F I am cheerful with an appropriate sense of humour.	☐	☐	☐

Based on material © Warwickshire LEA

OBSERVATION FORM

Teaching assistant _____

Observer _____ Date _____

What is the teaching assistant doing?	How is this helping the individual, group or the class teacher?

What evidence is there that the teaching assistant is helping the children and teacher meet the lesson objectives

Areas that are successful	Areas that need to be developed, and which could be future targets and future training needs

Signed _____ [teaching assistant]

Signed _____ [observer]

Date _____

SCHOLASTIC

REVIEW MEETING SUMMARY

Teaching assistant _____

Team leader _____ Date _____

Summary of the meeting including all areas of discussion

Signed _____ [teaching assistant]

Signed _____ [observer]

Date of next review meeting _____

Based on material © Warwickshire LEA

TARGET SETTING FORM

Teaching assistant _____

Team leader _____ Date _____

Target	Relevant notes/reasons/interim review dates

Signed _____ [teaching assistant]

Signed _____ [team leader]

Date _____

TRAINING AND DEVELOPMENT NEEDS

Training and development to develop the targets	What effect will the training and development have on raising standards in the classroom?

Signed _____ [teaching assistant]

Signed _____ [team leader]

Date _____

WORKING IN TEAMS

INTERPERSONAL SKILLS FOR EFFECTIVE TEACHING ASSISTANTS' ROLES

This chapter will explore some of the things that make schools and the people who work in them effective and successful. It will also look at developing teams and team building, their link to how standards can be raised and how effective teaching and learning can take place. In simple terms, all this means is that children need and deserve the best people working with them. At the same time these 'best' people, as well as working effectively for the children, need to be able to work for the benefit of each class and for the good of the school. Teaching assistants must not be marginalised within this process and must be encouraged and included in the school's working teams. For example, if there is a team working on raising writing standards, it is important that teaching assistants, who will be supporting groups of children with their writing, should be included.

WHAT MAKES TEACHING AND LEARNING SUCCESSFUL?

The most effective schools don't have isolated teachers working solely in classrooms with closed doors, or teaching assistants who don't speak to each other or discuss what they are doing. Effective schools are places where *everyone* works together to raise standards and improve the teaching and learning that takes place. This is not without its problems, because there are many people who find working together difficult. It is also true to say that there are certain personal characteristics that allow for more successful teamwork, better working relationships and far less tension, stress and conflict with colleagues.

Working with children in classrooms and schools is not always a static experience, where daily routines exist forever. Schools are not places where coming to work each day will necessarily mean that similar things happen in the same orderly fashion, and where change doesn't really have any effect on daily schedules. Schools are full of excellent, well-managed and well-led structures and systems that have been developed to raise standards. Teachers plan their teaching and learning meticulously, but what is planned and taught is not always the same as what children learn. This can mean that there are

constant small changes necessary in each and every working day and sometimes, quite sudden, large-scale changes have to happen if it becomes obvious that there are better and more effective ways of working.

These changes are not just arranged to disrupt anyone's working practices – they happen because they are necessary. As a teaching assistant you need to have the flexibility to work in a team and not to be afraid of change. In fact to be a really good teaching assistant, it is important to embrace changes that are introduced for the benefit of children and their learning. In other words, the role of the job will change over time, and all staff in a school must work together and grow and change with the job they are doing.

There are also a variety of viewpoints that are related to how children learn, and these different opinions and theories can and do influence what happens in school. In recent years, there have been many frequent changes, and the job range of roles and expectations of teaching assistants have changed and developed accordingly.

THE NEED FOR SELF-EVALUATION

It is important that working teams do just that – work effectively together. This is not always easy. As well as developing interpersonal skills that allow this to happen, it is extremely important for each teaching assistant to be aware of their own strengths, their own skills and, of course, their own weaknesses.

Obviously, each school will have a role to play in developing the skills of its teaching assistants as part of their staff development and team-building programme. Local Education Authorities will also have to support their schools by providing some training and development opportunities. However, there is a need for you as a teaching assistant to question your own personal development needs. You need to reflect on your own practice and what you do in the classroom and for the school. Useful questions to consider are:

● What have I done in my job today?
● How effective was it?
● Am I actually doing a good job?
● How can I do a better job?

It is really a process of reviewing the work that has been done and looking for improvements.

Self-evaluation and self-reflection are, in fact, similar to certain parts of performance management, which was examined in Chapter 1. Performance management is part of an annual review and target setting cycle related to the work that has been done and the work that needs to be done in future. It is a process involving another professional. Regular personal reflection, however, is the hallmark of a genuine professional. It takes place all the time and is where you as an individual draw together all your current working practices.

SELF-EVALUATION IN PRACTICE

The process of self-evaluation should draw conclusions from what is currently happening in the classroom with children and link these conclusions to a growing knowledge of children's needs, current educational developments and what is currently being developed from your own School Improvement Plan (SIP).

The following example gives an idea of how as a teaching assistant you can use self-evaluation to develop new strategies and improve your effectiveness.

AN EXAMPLE OF SELF-EVALUATION

You are working with a child on a one-to-one basis several times each week. The child has difficulty starting work, staying on task, concentrating on it and completing it within a reasonable time span. You plan to try different approaches which will be informed by:
- your knowledge of this particular child and his or her current problems
- your knowledge of previous children you have worked with
- your knowledge of what strategies and techniques have worked before
- any theoretical knowledge you have of child development and relevant teaching strategies.

However, it is often the case that the child does not make progress and improve, and that the techniques you have tried have not worked very effectively.

The next stage, therefore, could be to:
- share the problem with colleagues and discuss it with them
- read about similar cases and use further knowledge gained
- share your problems with your class teacher
- discuss the issue with a mentor.

This will mean that you will have:
- tried what you thought would work
- reflected on what happened
- discussed the issue further
- hopefully developed some new strategies.

This example shows almost a cycle of self-evaluation, which in many ways is similar to the performance management cycle looked at in Chapter 1. Yet at the same time, it demonstrates a willingness on the part of you, the teaching assistant, to analyse what is happening and to make improvements. In other words, it is centred on the importance of you yourself making structured changes to raise standards and improve the quality of teaching and learning.

WAYS TO SELF-EVALUATE

Some other important ways in which you as a teaching assistant can reflect on your own performance will include:

● Being prepared to talk with teachers and other teaching assistants about what is happening in the classroom in professional terms that relate to how improvements can be made.
● Reading about education, teaching and learning.
● Discussing new developments with colleagues – both other teaching assistants and teachers.
● Attending staff development events.
● Developing a critical approach to your work and analysing its successes and failures.
● Continuing your professional development through outside courses.
● Using performance management as an opportunity to set targets that are related to self-evaluation.

CHARACTERISTICS FOR WORKING SUCCESSFULLY WITH COLLEAGUES

Working with colleagues can be a minefield of egos, personalities and status. Positive relationships with colleagues are important and will influence the smooth running of the school and the effectiveness of teaching and learning. All professionals need to look at how relationships work and, if there are problems with conflict, how these can be minimised. There are various lists of attributes and working behaviours that are examples of good practice (some have already been touched on in Chapter 1), but if relationships between colleagues are to continue to be positive, everyone will need to:

● spend time reflecting
● discuss issues with colleagues
● recognise new ideas that are worth looking at
● be aware of what is happening in education, both locally and nationally
● have faith in colleagues' abilities
● be optimistic and positive
● be imaginative
● refuse to be complacent
● be good at listening
● enjoy other colleagues' accomplishments
● be a good communicator
● be open-minded and supportive.

INTERPERSONAL SKILLS

There are certain behaviour patterns of both individuals and groups, as well as specific contentious situations, that will determine whether professional relationships will be positive and effective or not. An interesting starting point for you as a teaching assistant could be to look at how you relate to groups of colleagues. Teaching assistants are important, both as individuals and as cogs in the school machine. How you work, behave and react with colleagues, and with the children that you teach, will have a bearing on how effective the school is. Where changes have to take place, for example to planning, to lesson structures or to which age range of children you will be working with, you will be more effective and successful if you can generate the professional enthusiasm to feel good about these, and if you and your colleagues are able to present a united front and work together.

In *Creating the Effective Primary School* (Kogan Page), Roger Smith looks at the characteristics that can determine good working relationships. He suggests common features that should bind colleagues together and make working relationships and, therefore, the school more effective. He points out that:

> …it is surprising how many colleagues that you work with will not have the interpersonal skills to take full advantage of working together within groups of people who share these sophisticated qualities… ' (page 35).

For teaching assistants, as much as any other professional colleague, interpersonal skills are important. If they are not present, it is not only the quality of relationships and the working ethos between colleagues that will suffer. I would argue that the quality of teaching and support will also be harmed, which means that children will not be getting the quality of education that they deserve and need.

SELF-RECOGNITION EXERCISE

In order to develop good interpersonal skills it is important to know your own strengths and weaknesses. Looking at yourself as an individual is not always easy, but try this activity. It asks you to look at yourself and take decisions about the following:

● How you really feel about yourself when you are working *[R]*
● How you would like to feel when you are working *[L]*

In other words, how you are and how you would like to be as a teaching assistant.

You will need to rate yourself on the 'Self recognition chart' (photocopiable page 38) using the following rating scheme, writing *R* against points 1 to 5, where 1 = good and 5 = poor. In the example below, the person sees themselves as quite a fair person.

Fair	1	2 *R*	3	4	5	Unfair

You will need to rate yourself against all the criteria on the chart before going on to the next stage.

When you have completed the chart, start from the beginning again and this time, rate yourself on how you would ideally like to be in your teaching assistant role by writing *L* at the appropriate place on each line. For example, if you see yourself as quite fair, but ideally would like everyone to think you were very fair, this part of the chart would probably look like this:

Fair	1 *L*	2 *R*	3	4	5	Unfair

ANALYSING YOUR SELF-RECOGNITION CHART

When you have completed the self-recognition chart it is important to look at the discrepancies. How large and important are the differences between how you feel you perform as a teaching assistant *[R]* and how you would ideally like to be performing *[L]*? Write down the four main significant differences that you have identified on your chart. The example below shows four such differences. For example, the first difference shows that the person thought that they were quite a solitary worker *[R]* but would ideally like to be more gregarious in their role *[L]*.

1. I am quite solitary in my job *[R]*, but would like to be more gregarious *[L]*.
2. I am rather sceptical in my job *[R]* and would like to be more trusting *[L]*.
3. I am nervous in my job *[R]* and would like to be more relaxed *[L]*.
4. I tend to be a little lazy in my job *[R]* and would prefer to be harder working *[L]*.

It is important to recognise the differences on the self-recognition chart and to take this just one step further. In a final exercise, suggest ways in which these discrepancies might affect your working relationships. For example, there is little point in working in a school if you prefer to be on your own. Team work

and solving problems co-operatively is the cornerstone of a successful school. Similarly, as a teaching assistant you need to be as assertive as possible within an atmosphere of trust. There is no place for the lazy, but plenty of support for anyone who is willing to be hard working in a relaxed and un-stressed way.

KEY INTERPERSONAL CHARACTERISTICS

The self-recognition chart should, if you were honest about your responses, have highlighted what you feel are your key characteristics. If you look at where you responded with an *[R]* on the chart it is possible to recognise your key characteristics. This is like a starting position and how you develop these characteristics into something more effective will help you respond more effectively within the school's working teams.

Roger Smith in *Creating the Effective Primary School* (Kogan Page) states that characteristics that determine good working relationships include:

- the approachability of all staff to other colleagues, children, parents, and so on
- appreciation of other people's point of view
- understanding and concern for the welfare of colleagues
- sympathy towards the views of colleagues
- the ability to inspire trust in colleagues
- tolerance of other people's ideas
- a sense of humour
- the ability to share problems and help solve them
- the willingness to praise and accept praise
- the ability to listen and to be tolerant
- being able to face up to conflict and to work to reduce and remove the source of the conflict
- knowing when to set tight deadlines and when to minimise pressure on colleagues
- the ability to be fair and just and to be seen to be fair and just
- knowing when to be part of the working team and when to lead, cajole, persuade and pressurise
- the ability to continue to be enthusiastic despite any conflict and problems (page 35).

UTILISING KEY CHARACTERISTICS

It is no good expecting that all your colleagues will be like you, because they won't. In fact, the better and more exciting the school, the more diverse the characteristics of the people working in them. Each teacher and each teaching assistant will have different personal quirks, and to counteract these differences, it is important that the working framework of the school is as consistent as possible. There will be policy documents for most areas of the school life as well as ways of identifying good practice and making sure that it is used across the school. As a teaching assistant, you will work within policy guidelines and you will be a supportive part of the school's management. In other words, you will need to have the positive personal characteristics to support what the school is doing.

Read each of the following characteristics and statements. For each one think about how it applies to you as a teaching assistant. More importantly, consider what you have done recently that 'proves' that you possess this characteristic and are able to use it to support teaching and learning.

> **Self-awareness**: You are aware of your own attitudes and values and how they affect other people within the school.
> **Will to achieve**: You constantly and willingly accept new challenges.
> **Optimism**: You feel positive about the future of the school and the part you intend to play in it.
> **Positive regard**: You respond to your colleagues with warmth, support and respect.
> **Trust**: You are prepared to trust colleagues.
> **Empathy**: You are able to understand (and this doesn't always mean agreeing with) colleagues' points of view.
> **Courage**: You are prepared to take appropriate risks to find more effective ways of working with children and colleagues.

There is a need for schools to emphasise what they think are 'good' personal characteristics, and to formalise how they feel teachers and teaching assistants should behave in their relationships with each other and with children (working with children will be the focus of other chapters). It should be possible to create a cohesive set of criteria for identifying the kind of good practice that will improve attainment and reduce any negative effect that poor and ineffective personal characteristics will have on teaching and learning and on how colleagues are able to work together. The following descriptions of 'bad' and ineffective practice are provided so that they can be avoided, because if they

exist and persist they will act as barriers to change and will lower a school's chance to raise standards and improve achievement.

A poor teaching assistant, who is likely to be ineffective, is one who:
- frightens children and acts as a kind of adult bully
- creates tensions with the children by setting unrealistic goals and deadlines
- sees children and parents as threats, and views parental help and support in a negative light
- emphasises punishment rather than praise, stress and tension rather than calm and hardly ever relaxes, smiles or laughs
- builds up relatively petty incidents out of proportion
- often sees lively and curious children as a threat and stifles enthusiasm
- sees education in terms of a narrow range of basic skills and frowns on a wide and creative curriculum
- defines arts and other forms of spontaneous creativity as not being 'work'
- has a suspicious attitude rather than an informed opinion towards change
- often 'insults' children and yet expects good manners and tolerance.

WORKING IN TEAMS TO MINIMISE CONFLICT

I need to repeat what has been said many times before. Everyone's individual personal, social and professional skills have to work both for the individual and for the team. The most effective schools will have staff with high quality interpersonal relationships. However, to work as a successful whole there will be various teams of colleagues who will have developed a high level of collaboration and an ability to work towards consensus rather than developing situations that cause conflict.

Working in a school as a teaching assistant should mean that you would be joining a working group where collaboration and consensus are the norm. But, as everyone knows, working with other people is fraught with hidden and not so hidden difficulties. Working together will not happen without everyone giving it careful thought and lots of hard work. Charles Handy in *Understanding Organisations* (Penguin) suggests that teams ' …mature and develop. Like individuals they have a fairly clearly defined growth cycle.' (page 160).

THE ROLE OF TEACHING ASSISTANTS IN TEAMS

Even though as a teaching assistant you might feel that in the hierarchy of seniority, decision making and responsibility within schools you are nowhere near the top, you are still important members of different professional teams and the more that is understood about working together the better. But, just because a headteacher says that teaching assistants should be part of a team that looks at how best to support groups of children during the transition from Infant to Juniors, for example, don't think that this means simply sitting round a table agreeing quietly and taking a few easy decisions. Sometimes it can work like this, but more often it doesn't and it is important not to be surprised or disappointed when decisions are less easy to make than you think.

Handy suggests four stages of how groups can develop into the kinds of effective teams that will have a positive effect on teaching and learning. These

conflict because, as has been suggested throughout this chapter, knowing yourself and your strengths and weaknesses is professionally important. It is also useful to look at your colleagues in terms of how you feel that they may handle conflict. How they react may well govern how you react in order to minimise any problem situations.

NON-ASSERTIVE STYLE

Those adopting this style of behaviour means that they prefer not to tackle conflict and their behaviour is both unassertive and usually unco-operative. At worst, these people will withdraw from any potentially threatening situations but, if we are more sympathetic than we perhaps should be, it is possible for them sometimes to wait for a better time and a more appropriate opportunity to discuss an issue. If and when conflict does arise, some of their responses might be:

- 'Can we talk about it later?'
- 'That is really nothing to do with me.'
- 'I'd rather not get involved… '

AGREEING STYLE

This behaviour is usually unassertive, but reasonably co-operative. Those who adopt this style will ignore their own needs and concerns to satisfy and meet the needs of their colleagues. They will probably spend a lot of time agreeing when they don't really want to, as well as giving in to their colleagues' points of view and demands. Some of their responses in a conflict situation might include:

- 'Yes, I totally agree with you.'
- 'Yes, you've got a good point there and I agree with you.'
- 'Yes, you have certainly convinced me… '

COMPROMISING STYLE

This behaviour lies somewhere between being unassertive and being co-operative. Those adopting this style will work hard at finding ways to satisfy all parties who are in conflict with each other. They will usually make concessions and meet people halfway rather than insisting they get all their own way. Some likely responses in conflict will include:

- 'I could agree with you there if you would accept that… '
- 'Let's see if we can agree on some things.'
- 'If we can agree on this we should be able to find a quick solution.'

COMPETITIVE STYLE

This style of behaviour means behaving in an assertive and rather unco-operative way. Those adopting this style will use their own power and expertise to pursue their own concerns in any conflict situation. This will usually mean that they will either attempt to win, defend their own position or stand up for their own rights. Their responses could include:

- 'Let me make my position quite clear.'
- 'Look, I know my way is the right way.'
- 'If you don't agree with this I will have to… '

PROBLEM-SOLVING STYLE

This style of behaviour is where someone is both assertive and co-operative. They will aim to resolve a conflict by reaching a solution that tries to satisfy everyone. To adopt this style they will need considerable interpersonal skills, honesty and a willingness to listen to different points of view. Responses might include:

- 'I feel this way about this problem... how do you feel?'
- 'Let's work out how we can solve this.'

Obviously, it is possible to operate within all the suggested styles at one time or another, and for different reasons and different problems. It is sometimes necessary to say 'Yes I totally agree with you' and equally, it is sometimes important to make the very clear statement that 'I know my way is the right way'. As a teaching assistant you may well be drawn into educational issues that you either know very little about or don't feel that you have the expertise or status to take part. If this were the case then saying 'This is really nothing to do with me' would be a reasonable, but not terribly helpful, response. Having said that, however, it should be clear that the problem-solving style above is the most appropriate way in which professional colleagues should relate to each other.

CONCLUSION

Conflict, and any subsequent breakdown in relationships, will make the school less effective. A less effective school means that the job of teaching assistant will also be less effective, less productive and more difficult to do. If the quality of relationships within the whole school and between colleagues is poor, negative, unhappy and unproductive, then what happens in classrooms with children is likely to be unsuccessful, leading to a fall rather than a rise in standards.

set and seems to be responding differently from the majority of children. According to the Code of Practice, the triggers for intervention are that the child:

● makes little progress, even when teaching approaches are targeted particularly in a child's identified area of weakness

● shows signs of difficulty in developing literacy or mathematics skills which result in poor attainment in some curriculum areas

● presents persistent emotional or behavioural difficulties which are not ameliorated by the behaviour management techniques usually employed in the school

● has sensory or physical problems and continues to make little or no progress despite the provision of specialist equipment

● has communication and/or interaction difficulties and continues to make little or no progress despite the provision of a differentiated curriculum.

The SENCo will begin to take the lead in further assessment and together with the class teacher should decide on the action needed to help the child to progress. The intervention strategies at the school action level will depend on the individual child, but regular discussions between parents and all those people who work with him or her is essential so that evidence can be gathered to identify the best and most effective course of action. Many teachers have an expectation at this level that help will take the form of the deployment of extra staff to enable one-to-one tuition to be given to the child. There are other approaches which may be more appropriate but will still involve the input that can be provided by a teaching assistant. Different learning materials or special equipment might be needed, for example, or some group work linked to individual support might be more useful.

One of the most important things that the teacher and teaching assistant must do at this level is to collect all kinds of evidence about the child that will be useful for the SENCo to use in writing the child's Individual Education Plan (IEP). The IEP should include information about:

● the short term targets set for or by the child

● the teaching strategies to be used

● the provision to be put in place

● when the plan is to be reviewed

● success and/or exit criteria

● outcomes (to be recorded when the IEP is reviewed).

There is an example of an IEP on photocopiable pages 58 and 59. Ideally, they should be reviewed at least twice a year with input from both parents and the child, where this is appropriate.

School Action Plus

This is the level of action that occurs immediately after an IEP review, when it is recognised that a child requires some support from outside the school. School action plus implies that the school has used several intervention strategies but now feels that there needs to be further provision provided by someone outside the school who has some specific expertise that will help the child. Most LEAs have support agencies that can be used, but there is a wide range of other services, which might include:

- the school nurse
- speech therapists
- social workers
- educational psychologists
- health visitors
- SEN advisory teams
- support units for particular disabilities

When schools seek the support of external support agencies, those services will need to see the child's records as well as their IEPs so that they know which strategies have already been used and which targets have already been set and achieved. Whatever outside support is needed, it is unlikely that it will be for the whole of any week. In fact, the support will be measured in hours, or at the most, a day or two each week. What this means is that both teacher and teaching assistant will have to be kept informed of the content of any new IEP and be able to follow up in class the work that will have either been started or suggested by the outside support agency.

Statutory assessment

Approximately two per cent of children will need to be provided with a statement of Special Educational Needs. This is a legally binding document that is reviewed annually. It describes the child's needs, the kind of support that must be put in place and how progress will be monitored. It is possible for children who have statements to be allocated a specific sum of money which must be used to meet their educational needs.

The Code of Practice is very clear on what evidence the school should have when they are asking for the kind of statutory assessment that could lead to a child being allocated a statement. The information should be about:

- the school's action through School Action and School Action Plus
- individual education plans for the pupil
- records of regular reviews and their outcomes
- the pupil's health including the child's medical history where relevant
- National Curriculum levels
- attainments in literacy and mathematics
- educational and other assessments, for example from an advisory specialist support teacher or an educational psychologist
   views of the parents and of the child
- involvement of other professionals
- any involvement by the social services or education welfare service.

Most children with statements will be able to function effectively in mainstream schools, providing they have the appropriate amount of support. Sometimes, that support will consist of a full time teaching assistant who is employed by the school to work with a statemented child. Teaching assistants who do this kind of intervention might be required to:

- Assist in the description of the child's learning difficulties.
- Be part of the provision of support.
- Specify the kind of teaching that is required, such as small group work or specific work in phonics.

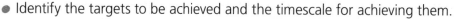

- Identify the targets to be achieved and the timescale for achieving them.
- Suggest how progress will be monitored and assessed.
- Set meeting times for parents, including the IEP review date.

It will be obvious from the various stages of SEN that a child has a learning difficulty if they:

- have a significantly greater difficulty in learning than the majority of children of the same age, or
- have a disability which prevents or hinders them from making use of educational facilities of a kind generally provided for children of the same age.

AREAS OF SPECIAL EDUCATIONAL NEEDS

The 2002 'Code of Practice' identifies four areas of SEN that can be used to look more closely at what would be expected of teaching assistants in a mainstream school. These areas are:

- Cognition and learning difficulties.
- Emotional, behavioural and social difficulties.
- Communication and interaction difficulties.
- Sensory and/or physical difficulties.

A child may, of course, have problems in more than one area. For example, a child may have a learning difficulty as well as an emotiona,l behavioural or physical problem.

It is important to look at each of these four areas in more detail.We should perhaps note that working with children who have emotional and behaviour difficulties (EBD), can involve some very precise and structured work with individual children that will involve techniques that are only applicable and useful for supporting identified children and, in the majority of cases, will not overlap as techniques and strategies that could be used with other children in the class. Working with children who have general areas of learning difficulties, such as learning to read at a slightly slower rate or having less of an understanding of number bonds than their peers, often involves techniques that can be used for all kinds of groups of children. Many of these classroom 'tricks of the trade' will be discussed later in the book and can be used for a variety of teaching and learning situations.

COGNITION AND LEARNING DIFFICULTIES

The two main areas that fall under this heading are general learning difficulties and specific learning difficulties.

GENERAL LEARNING DIFFICULTIES

These may occur in up to 18 per cent of any group of children at any one time. Children with these kind of difficulties may show:

- low levels of attainment in all forms of assessment, including base line assessment in their first year in school
- limited attention span
- difficulty in acquiring skills, especially in literacy and numeracy, on which much other learning in school depends

● difficulty in dealing with abstract ideas and generalising from experience
● associated difficulties related to speech, language and social and emotional development.

In simple terms, children who have general learning difficulties learn more slowly than others for a variety of often quite complex reasons. Although each child will have individual needs, and it is unwise to generalise, there are some fundamental areas of support that you will be involved in as a teaching assistant linked to children with general learning difficulties. These include support in the following areas:

● Practical work and concrete examples, involving more use of practical apparatus than is necessary for most children.
● Repeating and revisiting areas of learning.
● Frequent basic skills teaching, such as phonics, punctuation and number.
● Raising self-esteem and confidence building skills.
● Social skills.

Some children who have persistent general learning difficulties which limit their access to the curriculum, teaching and learning will have statements of Special Educational Needs. But all children who fall into this category will need consistent teaching assistant support. The following example suggests the level of support that a child with general learning difficulties should have if they are to be helped make improvements in their learning.

EXAMPLE OF SUPPORT FOR A CHILD WITH GENERAL LEARNING DIFFICULTIES

George has an SEN statement and the teaching assistant's time during the week is divided in the following way:

● Three hours each week supporting him in numeracy and literacy by working towards his targets on his IEP.
● Two half-hour sessions of one-to-one time, where the time is used to meet any specific social needs that have arisen during the week or to work on specific skills that have been identified as currently important by the class teacher.
● Two half-hour sessions within a small group of children experiencing similar difficulties. These sessions focus on the development of phonics, spelling and writing skills.
● The Educational Psychologist visits George once a term and discusses issues with both the class teacher and the teaching assistant.

SPECIFIC LEARNING DIFFICULTIES

These learning difficulties are those related to a relatively narrow, specific and focused area, such as dyslexia or dyspraxia. These are complex and difficult areas where support from outside the school is often needed to complement the work of the teacher and teaching assistant. Many children with specific learning difficulties have an identifiable mismatch between what they know and understand, and what they are capable of communicating by speaking or writing. Many children who are identified as having some form of dyslexia have good verbal ability, but their spelling, reading and writing is poor. This will mean that they need help with phonics, letter formation and all kinds of visual, auditory and kinaesthetic strategies. Most children with a specific learning difficulty are likely to have problems in one or more of the following areas:

- Difficulties with fine or gross motor skills.
- Signs of frustration and/or low self-esteem, taking the form in some, if not many cases, of behavioural difficulties.
- Inconsistent attainment, such as better oral and verbal work than written work or better drawing and visual skills than written ones.
- Low attainment in a specific curriculum area, especially in aspects of literacy or numeracy.
- Language difficulties, such as limited skills in verbal exchanges, following instructions and understanding concepts.
- Difficulties in tasks such as sequencing and those requiring good short-term memory.

Teaching assistants have a huge part to play in supporting children with specific learning difficulties. Many such children will be at Stage 3 on the school's Special Educational Needs Register and by being classified as School Action Plus will be receiving support and advice from outside agencies. The following list outlines some of the skills that teaching assistants will have to use and develop to support these children:

- Making sure that the children know their abilities are valued.
- Tackling any feelings of frustration and lack of confidence immediately.
- Helping the children to develop strategies for remembering information.
- Processing small chunks of information with the children because this will help them learn more effectively.
- Reading information to the children to help them overcome their difficulty with print.
- Encouraging other learning skills that they are good at.
- Providing the appropriate resources and helping the children use them effectively to access the curriculum, such as laptops and tape recorders.

The example below suggests the kind of individual support that a child with specific learning difficulties might need, if their difficulties are to be addressed effectively.

EXAMPLE OF SUPPORT FOR A CHILD WITH SPECIFIC LEARNING DIFFICULTIES

Fara is a bright, articulate girl who has severe problems with reading and spelling. As she moves up the school she is becoming more frustrated and her behaviour is beginning to suffer. A visiting specialist teacher has offered advice for the targets on her IEP and the same visiting teacher has trained a teaching assistant in a specialist programme of work that should support Fara's learning.

The teaching assistant will need to:

- Work with Fara on a specific spelling and phonics programme for 20 minutes each morning starting at 9am.
- Work alongside Fara during each Literacy Hour.
- Spend a total of one hour each week in one-to-one sessions involving phonics and spelling.
- Meet with the SENCo and the class teacher once each week to discuss progress and to plan future work.
- Meet with the outside specialist teacher once each half term.

EMOTIONAL, BEHAVIOURAL AND SOCIAL DIFFICULTIES

Children with emotional and behavioural difficulties (EBD) are often the most difficult to support and can cause the most disruption within the classroom. Many, but not all, of the techniques described here are specific to EBD children and will not necessarily be of much use to a teaching assistant who is working with a wider range of classroom learning issues.

Children who can be classified as having EBD usually show the following characteristics:

- Their behaviour can be age-inappropriate, or it can seem inappropriate or strange in other ways.
- Behaviour that they display, such as persistent calling out in class, refusal to work or persistent annoyance of peers, interferes with their own learning and that of other children in the class.
- Signs of emotional problems, such as tearfulness, withdrawal from social situations or temper tantrums.
- Difficulties forming positive social relationships and isolating themselves from their peers by, for example, being aggressive.

Children who exhibit difficult behaviour over a period of time will need support within the classroom from teachers, teaching assistants and visiting specialist teachers or other support agencies, such as educational psychologists. With effective support, these children will be able to remain within the mainstream classroom. Without it, such children will be difficult to fit into any school's inclusion programme because of their capacity for disrupting the teaching and learning that should be taking place.

THREE

RECOGNISING EMOTIONAL, BEHAVIOURAL AND SOCIAL DIFFICULTIES

It is important to look closely at the differences between a child with EBD and a child who works normally within the classroom with little or no support. The 'Child behaviour charts' (photocopiable pages 60 and 61) can be used as a good starting point to recognise differences in patterns of behaviour. This will be useful for you as a teaching assistant, as it should ideally be completed by a teacher and teaching assistant working together. It is, however, possible to be completed alone.

First think of a child who is usually seen as being perfectly 'normal' in classroom situations. Use 'Child behaviour chart 1' and write their name in the section 'Name of child 1' and then read each statement, ticking the box under the appropriate number. The scores on the chart equate to:

● +2 means a very positive pattern of behaviour.
● −2 means a very negative type of behaviour.

Secondly, think of a child who has EBD. Use 'Child behaviour chart 2' and write their name in the space alongside 'Name of child 2' and then tick the appropriate boxes, preferably using a different colour.

When the charts have been completed for both children, it is important to look at the differences in terms of why they should occur. Some of the questions that can be asked, and which will be part of this and later sections in the book, are:

● Why are there differences in behaviour?
● What are the differences in family background of the two children?
● Are these differences significant? If so, in what way?
● Are the two children treated differently in the classroom?
● What support does the child with EBD need so that inclusion is effective?
● Is the child with EBD getting this support?
● What effect does the child's EBD behaviour have on the rest of the class?

MANAGING EMOTIONAL, BEHAVIOURAL AND SOCIAL DIFFICULTIES

EBD pupils can be, and usually are, time consuming. As a teaching assistant you will need to be aware of a whole range of problems and behaviour issues that will range from mild attention seeking to the kind of defiant tantrums that will involve the teacher, and sometimes other senior managers, such as the headteacher. At the same time, there are also a whole range of strategies that can be used to minimise disruption and, if used consistently, modify the behaviour of a child with EBD.

In order to support the class teacher effectively, it is important that as a teaching assistant you are used to help analyse EBD behaviour and to match behaviour against the appropriate action that can be taken. Action is no use unless there is a point to it. In other words, it should be part of a strategy of behaviour modification rather than just a spur of the moment reaction that has no long-term effect. But, I have to say, it is sometimes necessary to prevent certain kinds of behaviour on the spot. For example, if a child with EBD was being physically or verbally abusive, instant action would be needed to stop the inappropriate behaviour immediately.

'BEHAVIOURAL PROBLEMS CHART' AND 'CHECKLIST OF POSSIBLE ACTION'

It is possible to try to match behaviour to preventative action. One way of doing this is to use the 'Behavioural problems chart' (photocopiable page 62) alongside the 'Checklist of possible action' (photocopiable page 63). These charts can also exist in their own rights as checklists to be used by both teachers and teaching assistants.

If you decide to use the charts together, it is probably most appropriate to use them for a specific child. First of all, think of a child with EBD who you are working with, and read through each of the behaviour problems on the 'Behavioural problems chart'. Tick all the boxes that are applicable to the child. Next, thinking of the same child, tick all the actions that you have tried on the 'Checklist of possible action' chart. Finally, in the space at the bottom of the 'Checklist of possible action' chart, make notes about successful and unsuccessful action. It is, after all, important not to waste time by using techniques that just don't work.

Both these charts and your notes can be used in meetings within the school to plan future actions, and with outside agencies. They will be especially useful in deciding targets for the child's IEP, and such charts can be used on a variety of children who have a variety of EBD problems.

STRATEGIES FOR DEALING WITH EMOTIONAL, BEHAVIOURAL AND SOCIAL DIFFICULTIES

Using the three charts, 'Behavioural problems chart', 'Checklist of possible action' and the 'Child behaviour charts', together with discussions between participants, such as the child, the child's parents, SENCo, teacher and teaching assistant, will make it possible to build up a picture of the kinds of issues that are prevalent within groups of children or individuals who have EBD. Identification, however, is relatively easy. Using the kinds of strategies that will modify emotionally disturbed behaviour, or even stopping it completely, is not easy. In fact it is time consuming, energy sapping and frustrating, and often a very long term rather than a short-term plan.

The 'Checklist of possible action' chart includes several strategies that can be used. Most teachers will try them and will expect you as a teaching assistant to support them in the classroom by developing the kind of skills that will allow them to use similar strategies. The most effective way of using these strategies, however, and this will apply to dealing with all kinds of behaviour issues and not just those associated with the severe problems caused by children with EBD, is if they are whole school strategies. In other words, the whole school, in terms of all teachers and teaching assistants, needs to agree that when rewards for positive actions fail, or when the child's behaviour towards another child, teacher or teaching assistant is very bad, then some kind of action or sanctions must be applied to stop the behaviour in the short term. Being positive and making efforts to change a child with EBD behaviour in the long term and with the support of outside agencies should not appear to condone bad behaviour or allow it to continue on a day-to-day and weekly basis. If this is allowed to happen it will affect the teaching and learning of other children. The wider needs of the whole class should not be superseded by the needs of a badly behaved child.

When using the 'Checklist of possible action', you will need to ask yourself the following questions:

● Which of the actions and/or sanctions should *I* be able to use effectively?
● Which ones should the *class teacher* use rather than me?
● Which ones are *whole school* strategies that *everyone* should use?

Before we leave this long section, which is more detailed than others precisely because children with EBD are the most difficult to deal with, let's identify four broad strategies within which the narrower and more immediate strategies of the 'Checklist of possible action' chart can be used more effectively. These four broad strategies are essential in working with EBD children, but can be used where other incidents of inappropriate behaviour occur.

1. BEHAVING POSITIVELY

Children with EBD are often attention seeking and they will behave in ways that mean they will get the attention of the teacher or teaching assistant in one way or another. The usual cycle is:

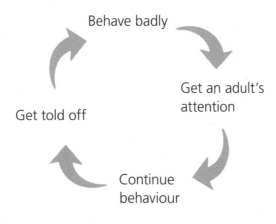

It might be worth trying a positive approach, where the child is praised and their self-esteem raised *before* they behave badly and before things start to go wrong. At the same time swift and sudden action needs to be taken to remove the child from their public (the rest of the class) when they behave badly. This should be done quietly, giving the child as little attention as possible, and it should be consistent and should happen every time. The message the child gets is that if they behave in a certain way, certain things will happen every single time.

2. TACKLING PROBLEMS IN A REALISTIC WAY

The point needs to be repeated – it is impossible to change a child with EBD into a model pupil overnight. It is a long-term problem and the solutions take skill, hard work, commitment and time. A realistic approach would be to arrange with the class teacher to tackle one problem at a time. This will mean using similar charts to the ones included here to analyse the problems that are the most important, to balance this analysis against the kinds of actions that have been taken and then adopting and maintaining a consistent approach which involves telling the child what will be happening and what the consequences of their inappropriate behaviour will be.

3. OFFERING PRAISE AND REWARDS

It is important that children understand that praise will be given and rewards offered for appropriate behaviour. In fact, in dealing with children at all levels, there must be more opportunities for rewards and praise than there are for sanctions and reprimands. All children, and especially those with EBD, need to know that their efforts and achievements have been worthwhile. It will help raise their self-esteem, which at best will be fragile, and at worst non-existent. It will be an important part of the teaching assistant's job to notice when children with EBD are being good and to praise them for it.

4. SHOWING CHILDREN WITH EBD WHAT GOOD BEHAVIOUR ACTUALLY IS

Children with EBD might not know what constitutes 'good' and 'appropriate' behaviour. One of the reasons for this is that no one at home has modelled this kind of behaviour. It is important that why their behaviour is inappropriate is explained to them, and at the same time that they are shown alternative ways of behaviour. Equally important is the fact that most inappropriate behaviour has at its cause some 'trigger point' that causes it to happen. If the trigger point can be found, it might be possible to prevent the inappropriate behaviour happening in future.

Some examples of common trigger points include:
- The child moving across the classroom between activities.
- Moving across the classroom to collect materials and resources.
- Sitting next to a particular child.
- Not being clear about what they have to do.
- Having to share resources.

The question that teaching assistants have to ask is what their part is in preventing these trigger points from happening. One of the ways to do this is to remember again that bad behaviour is learned. Children do not just invent and create it. This means that good behaviour is also learned and a teaching assistant is in a key position to 'model' the kind of good behaviour that a child with EBD needs to learn in order to function effectively in school.

Examples of this kind of behaviour modelling, which are linked to the list of possible trigger points, might include some or all of the following:
- 'Let me show you how to walk across the classroom.' [Demonstrate.]
- 'That is how I want you to reach across for the rubber.' [Demonstrate]
- 'You hang your coat up like this.' [Demonstrate.]
- When you want to answer a question, you put your hand up like this.' [Demonstrate.]
- Look how Olivia is sharing her book with Jessica. I want you to share yours with Sanjit like that.' [Uses another child's behaviour as a model.]

EXAMPLE OF SUPPORT FOR A CHILD WITH EMOTIONAL, BEHAVIOURAL AND SOCIAL DIFFICULTIES

Some statemented children have an amount of money allocated to them and this money can be used to provide the extra support that is necessary and appropriate. In this example, one-to-one support has been made available for a significant amount of time during the week.

David has an SEN statement that provides enough money for the school to use a teaching assistant just for him for eight hours a week. David has problems following the normal classroom rules on behaviour and he can be aggressive in his relationships with adults and other children. His work is below standard because of his constant disruptions and the fact that he finds it difficult to remain on task. The teaching assistant does the following:

- Spends five hours each week in literacy or numeracy, using the time to support David's learning and access to the curriculum, as well as

preventing his behaviour from disrupting his own learning and that of other children. This is agreed in advance with the teacher.
● Spends two hours in total working with a small group helping David to develop sharing skills and strategies for improving relationships.
● Has one hour put aside at the beginning of each week. It could be that it is an extra session in literacy or numeracy, or a further hour spent in developing group social skills. Sometimes it is a time set aside to withdraw David from the classroom for an hour to work on his self-esteem and talk him through some of the week's specific problems.
● Attends a meeting each term with outside support agencies. They help to develop a programme of suggestions that the teaching assistant can use, together with a report from an educational psychologist who will have monitored David in the classroom and talked to both him and his parents.

COMMUNICATION AND INTERACTION DIFFICULTIES

This is an extremely specialised area and teaching assistants must have specific skills and training to deal with children with these sorts of difficulties. It could be the case that a specialist teaching assistant would be used to support children with communication and interaction difficulties for some hours in the week, and for the rest of the time, more generalised support would be available. Children who need support in this category usually fit into two main areas: speech and language disorders and children with autistic spectrum disorders.

SPEECH AND LANGUAGE DISORDERS

This will usually mean that an individual child will need support in the classroom to help them understand what they are being asked to do, and to communicate their ideas to their peers and other adults. Obviously, this can be frustrating to the child and may lead to some interesting, complex and difficult patterns of behaviour, which will also need the attentions of a skilful teacher–teaching assistant partnership.

Children who fall into this category will have specific difficulties in the following areas:
● Speaking to their peers and to adults.
● Using the right words and creating sentences that can be both understood and are expressive and meaningful in the correct context.
● Understanding and responding to both the non-verbal and verbal cues of peers and adults.
● Gaining knowledge of, and being able to express, context appropriate thoughts and ideas.
● Understanding and being able to use the appropriate social language in the classroom, small groups and in non-structured situations, such as the playground.
These children will also display:
● The anxieties, frustrations and lack of self-esteem that arise because of the failure to communicate.

● The behaviour difficulties that manifest themselves because of the anxieties and frustrations and the deteriorating social and peer relationships.

EXAMPLE OF SUPPORT FOR A CHILD WITH SPEECH AND LANGUAGE DISORDERS

This example illustrates the kind of support that might be provided by a specialist teaching assistant who will have been trained in specific techniques.

> Adam has been placed at Stage 3 on the school's SEN register and there are discussions about the possibility of an SEN statement. He has significant speech problems which make it difficult for other children and adults to understand him. He has the support of a specialist teaching assistant for four hours each week. This has to be one-to-one support as Adam's speech problems are very specific. During the rest of the week a general teaching assistant, who works with children from the whole class and not just with Adam, supports him within the classroom.
>
> Specialist support is provided outside the classroom and is a programme devised by a speech and language therapist who visits every half-term to assess progress, monitor the support and suggest specific new approaches for Adam's IEP targets.

AUTISTIC SPECTRUM DISORDERS

This is an extremely difficult area to support and children who are classified as having this condition, which is often linked to Asperger's syndrome, are often frustrating because of their difficulties with social relationships, social communication and imaginative thought. Many children who are identified as being autistic have behaviour difficulties as well as difficulties accessing the whole curriculum. They often need continuous support, both in the classroom and in the playground. They may show:

● great difficulty in responding to social situations appropriately and to picking up normal verbal and non-verbal cues

● evidence of developing their own personal behaviour agendas which are not able to be directed by adults

● signs of withdrawal from certain social and educational situations by ignoring the activity, being totally passive about it, showing no initiative about taking part and sometimes by being defiant and aggressive if pressured to take part

● highly personalised and individualistic behaviour even when surrounded by 'normal' activities and play. This can manifest itself in repressed, reduced and inappropriate social interactions and an absence of awareness of the needs, demands and emotions of others

● a reduced need and a reduced potential for communicating with their peers or with adults. This may express itself in a limited and impaired use of language and/or in a strange and repetitive way of speaking with odd pitch and intonation

● obsessive or repetitive activities, which can range from how they move to what they say or what they are interested in

● anti-social behaviour, such as inappropriate shouting, moving around the room and violence towards peers and adults.

EXAMPLE OF SUPPORT FOR A CHILD WITH AN AUTISTIC SPECTRUM DISORDER

In this kind of example, the support not only helps the specific child learn but will also affect how they interact with adults and other children.

Tracey has an SEN statement for her autism and has full-time support from a teaching assistant for ten hours each week. For the rest of the time the same teaching assistant, who also has responsibilities for other work and other children in the class, supports her within the classroom.

The ten hours of support are organised around the targets on Tracey's current IEP and are aimed at developing social skills. They are usually conducted in small groups or as one-to-one and involve:

● Encouraging interaction with other children.

● Encouraging interaction with adults.

● Helping her understand how different children interact with each other.

There is a half-termly meeting involving the Educational Psychologist, SENCo, class teacher, teaching assistant and autistic support teachers to review work that has already been done and to move the IEP forward when this is appropriate. There is also a termly meeting with the educational psychologist, Tracey's parents and the class teacher.

SENSORY AND PHYSICAL DIFFICULTIES

As with the communication and interaction difficulties, those centring on hearing, vision and physical and medical difficulties present very significant problems for the class teacher and for the whole school. The educational and social demands may have to rely on specialist teaching assistants but, and this has been the case in earlier examples, it is unlikely that a full-time teaching assistant will be available or affordable. This usually means that if the child is going to be included in a mainstream class, they will have some specialist support and some more general support. Inevitably, if there are children with these difficulties in school, then most teaching assistants will have to be able to support them in some way.

HEARING IMPAIRMENTS

Hearing problems range from the relatively mild to the severe. In many LEAs there are specialist units for hearing impaired children, but many such children will be able to cope reasonably well in mainstream schools with support. If they can't, they will usually spend some time in a mainstream class before they are identified as needing the kind of very precise support that can only be given in a specialist unit. The problems associated with hearing impairment usually show up in some of the following ways:

● Clear physical changes, such as persistent earache and/or a discharge from the ears.

- The child may start tilting the head in certain directions to favour a particular ear or display an obvious concentration on the speaker's face during conversations or when instructions are being given.
- Increased reliance on instructions being given several times, or on peers helping by repeating or clarifying instructions.
- Deterioration in standard of work.
- Lack of response to whole class verbal cues and the need for one-to-one instructions.
- Frustration, which can lead to emotional and behavioural problems.

EXAMPLE OF SUPPORT FOR A CHILD WITH A HEARING IMPAIRMENT

The support that is suggested in the example opposite is not only about working with children to make improvements to their learning, but is also concerned with assessing difficulties so that appropriate support can be given to the children in the future.

There are two children in the class with hearing impairments. Amanpreet has an SEN statement and a teaching assistant for five hours each week. Elliot doesn't have an SEN statement, but is at Stage 3 on the school's SEN register and has a similar amount of support for five hours. The same teaching assistant is supporting both children and spends the rest of the week with the same class supporting the teacher in other ways.

Amanpreet has always worn a hearing aid and is overcoming many difficulties. She is trying and succeeding in working independently for much of the time and is beginning to resent having a teaching assistant working with her. Elliott, on the other hand, has only recently started to wear a hearing aid and his five teaching assistant hours (and some of Amanpreet's when she doesn't want or need any support) are spent:
- Assessing his full range of learning difficulties.
- Working in small groups in developing his social skills.
- Working on a one-to-one basis in developing his self-esteem.
- Working on tasks set by the hearing impaired support service.

There is a meeting every half term with a support teacher from the hearing impaired service who will set tasks for the teaching assistant based on the targets in Elliott's IEP.

VISUAL IMPAIRMENTS

As with hearing impairments, children who fall into this category may well need specialist support but, once again, this will not usually be for the whole week. This will mean that many of the child's needs will have to be met by the class teacher and teaching assistants who are allocated to the child and class.

If a child has a visual impairment there will usually be:
- Deterioration in such areas of work as handwriting.
- The obvious need for them to look closely at their own work and to squint at the whiteboard or struggle to see screens that are further away.
- Slowness in writing, especially when it involves copying from the board or from a book or worksheet.
- Asking for instructions to be given verbally, even if they are already available elsewhere in writing.
- Deterioration in hand–eye co-ordination in practical activities in subjects such as PE, design and technology and art.
- Anxiety, which can lead to refusal to try certain activities that require balance or moving around obstacles.
- Withdrawn and/or frustrated behaviour.

EXAMPLE OF SUPPORT FOR A CHILD WITH A VISUAL IMPAIRMENT

The support offered by the teaching assistant in the example overleaf is about taking advice from a specialist and then interpreting the kind of work that has to be done with the child.

Jake has his first SEN statement because of recently diagnosed sight problems. He has access to resources from the LEA visual impairment support service, such as a large keyboard laptop, and a teacher works with him on a one-to-one basis for one morning each week. He has ten hours of teaching assistant support each week and the same teaching assistant works with the rest of the class for the rest of the week. The teaching assistant's work consists of:

● Working on an arranged one-to-one programme organised by the visiting visual impairment teacher for three hours each week.

● Working alongside Jake in groups for five hours each week using aids that he sometimes has difficulty with, such as large print books or a special magnifying glass.

● Working in a small group on social skills that includes showing peers how to help Jake. For example, in making sure he has space on a table to put his large text version of the work they are doing.

There is a meeting each half term with the teacher from the visual support service to review progress and set new targets for Jake's IEP.

PHYSICAL AND MEDICAL DIFFICULTIES

There is an important issue here, and to a lesser extent it may apply to other areas of SEN. Many children with medical and physical conditions respond exactly as other children without their condition do to the teaching and learning environment. For example, a child who has to use a wheelchair may have a few problems relating to access to facilities, which should be easily overcome if their school is equipped and resourced properly, but they will otherwise be able to work and play effectively without SEN support. Only children whose medical and physical conditions prevent them from access to and engagement with the curriculum should be included in this category of difficulties. Examples could include children who have returned to school after a long absence through hospitalisation or children whose physical movement is impaired in some way that may prevent them having full access to the PE curriculum.

Conditions that are the most common will include:

● Evidence that the child has a learning difficulty.

● A physical or medical condition that affects self-confidence, self-esteem, emotional stability or relationship with peers.

● A disability that affects performance in the classroom because of lack of motivation, poor concentration, need to sleep and rest.

● A disability that affects access to play and subjects such as PE.

EXAMPLE OF SUPPORT FOR A CHILD WITH PHYSICAL AND MEDICAL DIFFICULTIES

This example is important because it includes suggestions as to the kind of support in PE that may be necessary for a child to access the whole curriculum.

Charlotte does not have a statement, but she is on the school's SEN register at School Action Plus. Charlotte lost her left foot in a car accident and now uses an artificial foot which, because she is growing quickly, has to be changed regularly. She has support from her class's usual teaching assistant for three hours each week.

The three hours are used in the following way:

- One hour's one-to-one work to maintain Charlotte's self-esteem and to work through any current problems, both social and academic.
- Two hours' support in PE and games.

This teaching assistant support is reviewed termly with the teacher, teaching assistant, SENCo and her parents, with the view that the support will eventually not be needed.

CONCLUSION

This chapter has tried to show the wide and varied nature of the range of Special Educational Needs in mainstream schools. There are more details in *How to Survive and Succeed as a Teaching Assistant* by Veronica Birkett (LDA, Cambridge) where she makes it clear that as a teaching assistant 'you will almost certainly be working with pupils who fit into one or more of the areas outlined… ' (page 21).

As a teaching assistant, you will often be involved in supporting individuals or small groups of children who may have particular problems with their work or behaviour. It is inevitable that some of these children will have been identified by the school as having Special Educational Needs. If this is the case, they will be on the school's SEN register and will be more closely supported and monitored than children who may still require support but do not need to be on the register.

There is a link between children's ability to learn confidently and access the whole of the curriculum, and their chances of reaching their appropriate level of achievement. Helping children to learn effectively is a necessary part of a teaching assistant's role, and that is why the rest of this book is concerned with the kinds of working practices, relationships, personal characteristics, teaching skills and learning techniques that will make working with colleagues and supporting children easier and more successful.

EXAMPLE OF AN INDIVIDUAL EDUCATION PLAN (IEP)

Name of child _____ Age _____ Date _____

Difficulties the child is experiencing.
Assessment information about the child, including teacher assessments and any national test results.
Learning targets for the next 6 weeks (no more than 3).
How will success and achievement be measured?
Action plan (who will do what and by when?)

CONTINUED...

EXAMPLE OF AN INDIVIDUAL EDUCATION PLAN (IEP) – CONTINUED

What extra input will there be?

How will progress be monitored?

Review

Date _____

Was the action plan carried through?

Were the targets achieved?

Information for future plans.

CHILD BEHAVIOUR CHART 1

Name of child 1 _____

Positive behaviour	+2	+1	0	1	2	Negative behaviour
Attends school regularly	☐	☐	☐	☐	☐	Misses school regularly
Has no physical illnesses	☐	☐	☐	☐	☐	Regularly has aches and pains
Is confident	☐	☐	☐	☐	☐	Lacks confidence
Appears happy at school	☐	☐	☐	☐	☐	Appears unhappy at school
Arrives at school on time	☐	☐	☐	☐	☐	Often arrives late
Has supportive parents	☐	☐	☐	☐	☐	Parents show little support
Responds well to discipline	☐	☐	☐	☐	☐	Responds badly to discipline
Responds well to praise	☐	☐	☐	☐	☐	Responds badly to praise
Is helpful to others	☐	☐	☐	☐	☐	Is unhelpful to others
Can work and play independently	☐	☐	☐	☐	☐	Is not independent
Can remain in seat in class	☐	☐	☐	☐	☐	Is often out of seat
Behaves well outside the class	☐	☐	☐	☐	☐	Behaves badly out of class
Is on task in class	☐	☐	☐	☐	☐	Is off task in class
Enjoys being on task	☐	☐	☐	☐	☐	Irritable and fidgets on task
Has good concentration	☐	☐	☐	☐	☐	Has poor concentration
Respects peers	☐	☐	☐	☐	☐	No respect for peers
Has good self control	☐	☐	☐	☐	☐	Lacks self control
Respects others' property	☐	☐	☐	☐	☐	Has no respect for others' property
Usually asks for help	☐	☐	☐	☐	☐	Waits for help to be provided
Moves from task to task easily	☐	☐	☐	☐	☐	Disturbs others between tasks
Settles down to work quickly	☐	☐	☐	☐	☐	Takes too long to settle
Copes with changes to routines	☐	☐	☐	☐	☐	Cannot cope well with changes
Can talk positively with an adult	☐	☐	☐	☐	☐	Talks negatively to adults
Likes to complete tasks	☐	☐	☐	☐	☐	Does not try to complete tasks
Is co-operative with adults	☐	☐	☐	☐	☐	Is unco-operative
Is fair to peers	☐	☐	☐	☐	☐	Is unfair to peers
Follows an adult's instructions	☐	☐	☐	☐	☐	Disobeys adults
Has one or more friends	☐	☐	☐	☐	☐	Has few friends
Is not aggressive with peers	☐	☐	☐	☐	☐	Fights with peers
Joins in playground games	☐	☐	☐	☐	☐	Plays alone
Is interested in other children	☐	☐	☐	☐	☐	Only interested in self
Is not a bully	☐	☐	☐	☐	☐	Is a bully
Is popular with peers	☐	☐	☐	☐	☐	Is disliked by peers

Based on material © Warwickshire LEA

CHILD BEHAVIOUR CHART 2

Name of child 2 _____

Positive behaviour	+2	+1	0	1	2	Negative behaviour
Attends school regularly	☐	☐	☐	☐	☐	Misses school regularly
Has no physical illnesses	☐	☐	☐	☐	☐	Regularly has aches and pains
Is confident	☐	☐	☐	☐	☐	Lacks confidence
Appears happy at school	☐	☐	☐	☐	☐	Appears unhappy at school
Arrives at school on time	☐	☐	☐	☐	☐	Often arrives late
Has supportive parents	☐	☐	☐	☐	☐	Parents show little support
Responds well to discipline	☐	☐	☐	☐	☐	Responds badly to discipline
Responds well to praise	☐	☐	☐	☐	☐	Responds badly to praise
Is helpful to others	☐	☐	☐	☐	☐	Is unhelpful to others
Can work and play independently	☐	☐	☐	☐	☐	Is not independent
Can remain in seat in class	☐	☐	☐	☐	☐	Is often out of seat
Behaves well outside the class	☐	☐	☐	☐	☐	Behaves badly out of class
Is on task in class	☐	☐	☐	☐	☐	Is off task in class
Enjoys being on task	☐	☐	☐	☐	☐	Irritable and fidgets on task
Has good concentration	☐	☐	☐	☐	☐	Has poor concentration
Respects peers	☐	☐	☐	☐	☐	No respect for peers
Has good self control	☐	☐	☐	☐	☐	Lacks self control
Respects others' property	☐	☐	☐	☐	☐	Has no respect for others' property
Usually asks for help	☐	☐	☐	☐	☐	Waits for help to be provided
Moves from task to task easily	☐	☐	☐	☐	☐	Disturbs others between tasks
Settles down to work quickly	☐	☐	☐	☐	☐	Takes too long to settle
Copes with changes to routines	☐	☐	☐	☐	☐	Cannot cope well with changes
Can talk positively with an adult	☐	☐	☐	☐	☐	Talks negatively to adults
Likes to complete tasks	☐	☐	☐	☐	☐	Does not try to complete tasks
Is co-operative with adults	☐	☐	☐	☐	☐	Is unco-operative
Is fair to peers	☐	☐	☐	☐	☐	Is unfair to peers
Follows an adult's instructions	☐	☐	☐	☐	☐	Disobeys adults
Has one or more friends	☐	☐	☐	☐	☐	Has few friends
Is not aggressive with peers	☐	☐	☐	☐	☐	Fights with peers
Joins in playground games	☐	☐	☐	☐	☐	Plays alone
Is interested in other children	☐	☐	☐	☐	☐	Only interested in self
Is not a bully	☐	☐	☐	☐	☐	Is a bully
Is popular with peers	☐	☐	☐	☐	☐	Is disliked by peers

BEHAVIOURAL PROBLEMS CHART

Name of child _____

Age _____ Class _____ Date _____

Behaviour	Tick if appropriate
Social isolation	☐
Aggressive attitude	☐
Attention seeking	☐
Bullying	☐
Immature play	☐
Withdrawn behaviour	☐
Anxious attitude	☐
Moodiness	☐
Seeming to be unhappy	☐
Running away	☐
Stealing	☐
Stuttering	☐
Constant talking in class	☐
Withdrawn behaviour	☐
Throwing equipment	☐
Giggling in class	☐
Damaging equipment or property	☐
Taking others' equipment	☐
Defiance	☐
Lying	☐
Swearing	☐
Stealing	☐
Excessive quietness	☐
Fearful	☐
Tearful	☐
Spitting	☐
Fussing over trivial complaints	☐
Shouting out	☐
Immature play	☐
Inappropriate noises, such as humming, pencil tapping	☐
Irritability	☐
Nervous twitches	☐
Lashing out and poking other children	☐

CHECKLIST OF POSSIBLE ACTION

Name of child _____

Age _____ Class _____ Date _____

Action	Tick if tried
Overlook or ignore the inappropriate behaviour	☐
Check for changes in the child's home background	☐
Check the child's health	☐
Look at and read all the child's records	☐
Discuss the child with the SENCo	☐
Check that there is the correct match between the child's ability and the work that has been set	☐
Avoid giving too much attention to the child's behaviour	☐
Alter the seating arrangements in the group or the whole class	☐
Discuss the behaviour with the child	☐
Encourage peers to ignore the disruptive behaviour	☐
Give the child the responsibility of a job to do	☐
Praise good behaviour	☐
Praise small improvements in their work	☐
Remind the child that you disapprove	☐
Reorganise the class by changing the groups	☐
Use a behaviour contract or personal behaviour chart	☐
Deprive the child of any special privileges	☐
Give the child extra work to do	☐
Send the child out of the room	☐
Send the child to another teacher	☐
Send the child to the headteacher	☐
Reprimand the child privately	☐
Arrange a detention	☐
Discipline the child in front of the whole group	☐
Keep the child in at break	☐
Keep the child in at lunchtime	☐
Exclude the child for a fixed term	☐

Notes

MANAGING CHILDREN'S BEHAVIOUR AND BREAKING DOWN BARRIERS TO LEARNING

Let's begin this chapter in the right frame of mind by not making any incorrect assumptions. It is not about 'bad' behaviour as such, nor does it concentrate on children whose behaviour is extremely inappropriate. It is more about developing consistent systems of control, having appropriate expectations and developing children's own positive attitudes. This chapter also looks at the importance of self-esteem in children, identifying barriers to learning and how to overcome them. All these issues are interlocking parts of the umbrella beneath which effective classrooms operate. Putting it more simply – no control, no teaching and learning.

SUPPORTING CHILDREN

As a teaching assistant, you will be involved with supporting children in the whole class, in groups and working with individuals. Less experienced teaching assistants who are supporting children will be relatively closely supervised by class teachers with regard to the nature of the tasks they can undertake with children. Experienced teaching assistants, however, with appropriate training may be given greater autonomy to identify suitable materials and manage agreed tasks. Managing children's behaviour is basically about making sure that all the children are part of the teaching and learning activities that are taking place, that they are all accessing the curriculum and that they all feel as positive as possible about each lesson and activity. Let's look first at some general principles of behaviour management.

SIMPLE STRATEGIES FOR SUPPORTING CHILDREN IN THE CLASSROOM

As a teaching assistant you will be involved in working alongside the class teacher when whole class teaching is taking place. Overleaf are some simple strategies that will help support all children and include them in the lesson. Many of these suggestions are very useful in both literacy and numeracy, but can also be used in any whole class lesson or part of a lesson.

DRAWING IN RELUCTANT CHILDREN

Sometimes there will be children in the class who are shy and reluctant to join in the lesson. As a teaching assistant it is possible for you to speak for them and give them the encouragement to speak. For example, saying 'You have a good idea haven't you Jake? Tell them Jake.'

SUPPORT DURING QUESTIONS AND ANSWERS OR CLASS DISCUSSIONS

Some children will be slow to start and slow to develop their ideas. It is important to start them off before they have missed out on the opportunity to contribute to class discussions. Saying, 'Sue, tell everyone about your holiday and all the interesting things you found on the beach' will help children to contribute successfully.

SUPPORT FOR SHY CHILDREN

Children lacking in self-esteem, or who may have learning difficulties of some kind, do not have the confidence to initiate a conversation or join in with an activity. They may only need the support that can be given by just smiling at them or nodding and giving them eye contact.

SPEAKING UP FOR CHILDREN

This is a useful technique when it is obvious that children haven't understood what the teacher is saying. You might have to ask for something to be explained more fully on behalf of the child. For example, 'I don't think Jane has quite understood that, could you go over it again?'

SUPPORT FOR CHILDREN NOT FOLLOWING THE LESSON

This is important and will mean watching children during the lesson and identifying who is daydreaming and not listening. If children are seen to be off task, a look, a gesture or a movement towards them is often all that is needed to start them concentrating on the lesson again.

REPEATING SPECIFIC PARTS OF THE LESSON

This will be important for many children who will only need the reassurance of someone double checking what has already been said. For example, 'Look Jamie, Mrs Cross is talking about paragraphs. We remember those from last week don't we?'

MONITORING BEHAVIOUR

It is important to know which children are disruptive and find it difficult to stay on task. Some of these children will have EBD, but some won't. Sitting close to such children may be enough, but it may also be necessary to quietly move them within the classroom or even take them outside to carry on working.

SUPPORT WITH EQUIPMENT

This will include making sure that everyone has what they need and is able to use it properly. For example, if the class are using protractors, or measuring precisely with centimetres and millimetres, there will be some children who will need help selecting the correct equipment as well as using it.

Whatever the situation you find yourself in as a teaching assistant, whether it is supporting children within the whole class, with a small group or when you are working with an individual child, you should receive support and guidance from the class teacher, the SENCo, a subject specialist or even an external support teacher or educational psychologist. This advice, together with your own personal and professional knowledge, which is of course invaluable, should mean that the skills you will develop would include:

● motivating children
● understanding and dealing with children's behaviour and attitudes
● encouraging independent learning and self motivation in children
● encouraging and developing children's self-esteem.

This chapter will concentrate on helping you develop these skills, but none of them will be as useful as they should be unless the children you work with have high self-esteem.

SELF-ESTEEM IN CHILDREN

Self-esteem is the value any individual gives to their own worth. If children have high self-esteem, they will place great value on themselves and will believe that they are worthwhile. This will mean that they are more likely to be creative and successful, and in social terms will be able to make and sustain good and lasting relationships.

On the other hand, children with low self-esteem will feel unworthy and will not value themselves. Because of this, they will quite often treat themselves, their peers and adults badly. This will have a negative effect on how they learn, how they behave and how they form relationships. Low self-esteem is the major cause of disaffection, lack of motivation, poor achievement and poor behaviour in children, and it is important to remember that all children, and especially those with low self-esteem, need encouragement, praise and rewards to motivate them to succeed.

RECOGNISING LOW SELF-ESTEEM

Children with low self-esteem are more likely to fail and are one of the major reasons for low educational attainment, low standards and the kinds of discipline problems that can have a detrimental effect on the quality of the teaching and learning that takes place in the classroom. Raising self-esteem is obviously very necessary and very, very important.

Recognising low self-esteem is equally important. The following list may well include some of the characteristics that have already been listed in Chapter 3 on EBD children. This is because most EBD children have low self-esteem. In fact, many children with all kinds of SEN have low self-esteem, which is another indication of how debilitating this can be within any classroom or any group of children, let alone how difficult it must be for the individual child. There is a longer list of signs of low self-esteem in children in *How to Survive and Succeed as a Teaching Assistant* by V Birkett (Cambridge, LDA), but some common signs will include:

- behaving defensively
- distrusting everyone
- fear of trying out new things
- making excuses for everything, including their own failures
- reluctance to complete work in case it is wrong
- constantly apologising
- anti-social behaviour
- being over critical of their own achievements
- being withdrawn or shy
- attention seeking
- teasing other children
- whining
- inability to make choices
- inability to take decisions
- blaming everyone else
- needing to win
- exaggerated boasting
- needing to be perfect
- trying to over please
- cheating in games.

If you still aren't convinced that raising self-esteem in children is important, there are also other issues surrounding such children. They will often, for example, think of themselves as 'thick' and say it out loud to adults and peers. This will make other children reinforce this opinion of themselves by repeating it back to them. They are also vulnerable to teasing, to being ostracised and to being bullied. Dennis Lawrence in

FOUR

Enhancing Self Esteem in the Classroom (Paul Chapman Publishing) suggests that:

> 'A vast body of evidence has accumulated showing a positive correlation between self-esteem and achievement and with regard to self-esteem and school achievement in particular... There is clear evidence that relationships between teachers (and this can include teaching assistants) and students can be either conducive to the enhancement of high self-esteem or conducive towards reducing self-esteem' (page 43).

STRATEGIES FOR RAISING SELF-ESTEEM IN THE CLASSROOM

Low self-esteem is a leading reason why standards can be difficult to raise, and thus a difficult problem to solve. But, if everyone makes it a whole school issue then it is possible to make fundamental changes.

So what do we do? Well, many of the strategies to raise self-esteem suggested below are well tried and are certainly not new, but they will work if they are applied and used consistently. They will also be useful in all kinds of other ways when working in the classroom.

When reading the strategies it will be useful to ask these questions:
- Do we use this strategy in school?
- Does everyone use it?
- Do I use it in the classroom?
- If I don't use it, why don't I?
- How can I use this strategy in future?

PRAISE MORE THAN YOU REPRIMAND

Try to give specific praise to a child with low-self esteem several times each day, and give praise for being brave enough to try something new. It is important to recognise successes by praise even if a target has not been reached.

REPRIMANDS SHOULD BE SHORT AND QUIET

Reprimand by labelling behaviour as undesirable, not the child, and use a quiet voice. Where possible, do this away from their peers and in private. Find an opportunity to praise a child as soon as possible after a reprimand by trying to say something positive to or about the child in everyone else's hearing.

SHOW THE CHILD YOU CARE ABOUT THEM

Try and learn something about the child's background so that you are able to ask personal questions about what is important to them, such as questions about their dog or cat, or their sick grandma. It is also important to smile and use a child's name. If a child goes into hospital, why not send a card?

HAVE AN APPROPRIATE PROFESSIONAL ADULT ATTITUDE

Be on time for your group or individual lessons with all the appropriate equipment. If you are not going to be there tell the children why. Say sorry if you make a mistake, and thank children for their contributions and for any jobs they have done. Try to give time to listen to what children want to tell you. It

might be very important to them and may give you a clearer understanding of the background to some aspects of their behavioural problems.

MAKE IT CLEAR WHAT IS AND IS NOT ALLOWED

All children need to feel that they are treated fairly and honestly and as individuals. They should not be compared unfavourably with another child. No one in the class should ever be allowed to say anything negative about anyone else. The classroom should ideally be a 'no put-down zone', where sneering and one-upmanship are not allowed.

MAKE SURE THE WORK AND TASKS SET ARE APPROPRIATE

The work that is being done should be differentiated in ways that make it appropriate for the individual child. The work should not be too easy or too hard. This is because each child will need to experience success. For a child with low self-esteem this might mean direct and tangible links with rewards and praise, through the use of stickers, certificates or charts.

There are further interesting suggestions for strategies for raising self-esteem in *Plans for Better Behaviour in the Primary School* by S Roffey and D O'Reirdan (David Fulton), pages 20–21.

ENCOURAGING INDEPENDENCE IN CHILDREN THROUGH SELF-ESTEEM

For the strategies to work, there has to be a certain amount of quite intense one-to-one support in the classroom. This kind of support is essential for some children, but as a teaching assistant you need to give support with the intention of making the child as independent as possible so that the support can be withdrawn at some point.

FOUR

It is important to recognise examples of the kind of support that will encourage independence ('appropriate support'), and the kind that may be fine in the immediate short term but which will not really help the child to develop their own skills and strategies ('inappropriate support'). Below are two examples of support given to a child, one an example of inappropriate support and the other an example of appropriate support.

> ### INAPPROPRIATE SUPPORT
>
> You are working with Sophie, who exhibits some of the classic behaviour characteristics of a child with low self-esteem. The class teacher's main concern at the moment is Sophie's inability to complete the work that is set, and the fact that when she does start the work her desire to be perfect means that, for example she will write a reasonable sentence, and then immediately try to erase it and find something better to write. At the same time, Sophie tries to belittle everyone else's work by teasing other children, inside and outside the classroom.
>
> Once Sophie accepts your support she wants to be with you all the time and wants you to help her make her work perfect. You are pleased that she accepts your support and encourage her attachment by working alongside her in the classroom, agreeing with her attempts at perfection and telling her to be quick and start again when she rubs her work out. More often than not, when you are worried that she is not producing any work, you will give her some ideas to write down. You also go out into the playground and act as an intermediary on her side when her teasing of other children erupts into conflict.
>
> This pattern of support means that the work that is produced in the classroom is more yours than hers, and that you are solving all her playground problems so that she is unable to recognise the consequences of her own teasing behaviour and the reasons why her friendships are either non-existent or very short lived. At the end of the year when she moves to another class she will have learned from your support that she is incapable of working independently. She will also be incapable of accepting that some of her ideas are better than others, and that it is important to recognise these good ideas and to write them down as part of her work. She will also have very few strategies for dealing with her peers in the playground. Because of your intervention in the playground she will not be able to understand that it is her behaviour that is causing the problems.
>
> By not understanding her own 'faults' she will not know the kind of behaviour that is unacceptable. When she joins her next class she will be at the same starting point as she was a year earlier and the support that she has received, which was largely expensive and intensive one-to-one support, has not been helpful in raising her self-esteem or improving her independence.

APPROPRIATE SUPPORT

The same child, Sophie, feels secure with you. You work closely with her and make sure that you value her skills and take an interest in her problems. You constantly let her know that you have high expectations of her. For example, when she is striving for perfection in a writing task, you make sure that she knows what she has to do and tell her to write two sentences to start with. Then you go and help someone else and come back to Sophie to look at what she has written. If it is good, you tell her, praise her and refuse to let her erase it and say that she doesn't like it. Equally, if it isn't good enough, agree with her, and instead of losing the original idea work with her on getting it right and then praise her for persevering.

You agree to be with her in the playground occasionally. When you witness her teasing, and other children's reactions to this, you work with Sophie to help her understand what she is doing that other children don't like and try to suggest better ways for her to behave. At the same time you also talk to the other children involved and try to explain to them what is happening, and how they could avoid reacting in ways which lead to conflict.

When Sophie moves up to her next class she should be more independent and able to make better judgements about the quality of her work. In the playground it is also possible that she will be able to recognise the kind of behaviour that causes problems and modify it. By being able to succeed more often in the classroom, and avoid conflict in the playground, her self-esteem may have improved over the year.

MANAGING CHILDREN'S BEHAVIOUR

Children don't, as you well know, arrive in the morning, learn quietly and placidly all day and then leave peacefully and go home. This is not how schools work – and I have to say, is not how a group of adults would behave either. The behaviour of the class has to be managed. There have to be discipline and control strategies that mean that all the children are managed in ways that encourage and allow teaching and learning to take place.

BARRIERS TO LEARNING

If you have not worked in schools before, or for very long, it will be useful to understand why children sometimes fail to respond to adults in ways that adults would like. There are predictable and unpredictable reasons, and both can seriously affect how learning takes place in the classroom.

More predictable barriers to a child's learning, that are usually known about before a child even arrives in the class where you are supporting learning, can affect behaviour and attitude. What these barriers are will have been passed on from the previous class teacher and learning strategies need to be available to overcome these most predictable of problems, which include:

- being slow to settle in class
- being easily distracted
- copying other children's work
- failing to complete homework
- preferring to gossip rather than listen
- not responding particularly well to praise
- completing work quickly and at a superficial level.

More unpredictable barriers to a child's learning can include:
- children having significant special needs
- poor attendance
- inability to accept rules and routine social constraints
- low self-esteem and a sense of failure
- poor socialisation skills
- lack of parental support
- family changes, such as divorce, separation and death
- lack of participation in anything that the school offers.

Some of these barriers to learning, such as lack of parental support, may prove to be intractable. Some, of course, are largely out of the school's hands. For example, a difficult divorce and separation that affects a child's learning and attitude can occur suddenly and can prove to be difficult to handle in the classroom. More often than not such incidents cannot be planned for and can only be managed successfully when both teachers and teaching assistants have a wide range of skills available to them.

CHILDREN'S ATTITUDES TO LEARNING

The attitudes that children bring to learning can be much more powerful than any innate ability and measurable intelligence, and can determine to a great degree their behaviour and how much they will benefit from the teaching that takes place. Obviously, children with positive attitudes to learning will:
- behave well
- get on with their peers

- relate well to adults in the classroom
- be interested in the work that they are asked to do
- be able to sustain concentration
- will always be involved in tasks set by the teacher.

In fact, they will be model children and every class will benefit from having them and the example they set to others.

Unfortunately, there will also be children with negative attitudes, and strategies will have to be developed to change these negative attitudes to positive ones. This is extremely difficult, but here are some of the negative attitudes that have to be overcome in order to raise achievement:

- an unwillingness to apply themselves to tasks
- a refusal to join in discussions
- an unwillingness to persevere with tasks or to solve difficult problems
- a lack of enthusiasm
- a lack of pride in their work
- difficulty in participating in group work, especially co-operative group work
- an inability to share resources, including their own and those belonging to the class
- an inability to learn from their mistakes
- hating to make mistakes of their own, but being quick to laugh at the mistakes of others
- an inability to work without the direct supervision of a teacher.

BREAKING DOWN BARRIERS TO LEARNING

Teachers and teaching assistants are at the centre of the process of breaking down barriers to learning. As a teaching assistant, you will work with teachers who are skilled, or who will become skilled, in using all kinds of strategies that they find will work.

FOUR

STRATEGIES FOR DISCIPLINE

In *You Know the Fair Rule* by B Rogers (Longman) three basic discipline types are suggested: Preventative, Corrective and Supportive. These are described below.

PREVENTATIVE DISCIPLINE

This is where there has been careful planning in terms of classroom organisation so that, for example, children whose behaviour is inappropriate are less likely to sit anywhere near similar children.

CORRECTIVE DISCIPLINE

This is when the teacher, or you as the teaching assistant, corrects children's behaviour and attitude in some way.

SUPPORTIVE DISCIPLINE

This is where the corrective side of the process of discipline is supported by follow-up work with the child. This could include an individually designed behaviour management chart and/or a reward and sanction system, so that supportive relationships are re-built and re-established through further contact with an adult, who may be either the teacher or you as the teaching assistant.

These three strands of classroom discipline are the basis of all effective behaviour management strategies. In applying them, there are four further underlying principles. These four key words could become every teaching assistant's classroom mantra: Clear, Calm, Consistent and Positive.

CLEAR

You will need to ensure that any rules of behaviour you have, and any requests you make related to how children behave, are clear and explicit and not open to any kind of misinterpretation. It should then also be clear when they are being followed and complied with and equally, when they are not.

CALM

You need to be in control of yourself and of every classroom situation. This does not mean being bland or faceless. Rather, it means giving children the sense that you will remain unflustered, whatever happens, and you will remain calm and firm under pressure. Each child needs to know that you are in control of the situation and that your relationship with them is based on creating a sense of professional, purposeful 'calm'.

CONSISTENT

One way of describing being consistent as a teaching assistant is to suggest that you should say 'yes' to children as often as possible, but when you say 'no' you mean it every single time. Another way of putting this is that you will mean what you say every time – without fail.

POSITIVE

You should be giving many more rewards than you are punishments. All your work with children should be based on focusing on their achievements and improvements, however small.

DISCIPLINE IN PRACTICE

The ideas of preventative, corrective and supportive discipline, being used in clear, calm, consistent and positive ways, needs to be pared down to some positive classroom activities. Here are some suggestions as to what tactics can be used in managing and supporting children.

MAKE IT CLEAR WHAT YOU WANT

The school and the class you will be working in will have rules and behaviour strategies that you will have to work to. However, it is important that you have a plan of action with any groups you are working with that makes it perfectly clear what you will and will not allow. Your children will need to be regularly reminded of the rules that you want them to keep to. These rules could include:

- Listen to other children when they are talking without interrupting.
- Don't leave your place without asking.
- Don't shout out answers.
- Don't snatch any shared resources.

HELP CHILDREN BE ASSERTIVE

This is not about you being assertive, but about helping shy, vulnerable children with low self-esteem to feel a sense of empowerment and to feel that they are in control. Teaching children to say what they feel and what they want to other children can help them in controlling their own frustrations, that in turn can lead them towards inappropriate behaviour. Help them to use 'I' statements in situations that they don't like. For example, 'I don't like you calling me names and laughing at me. I want you to stop doing it.' Children should be encouraged to use these kinds of statements and then walk away from the situation, preferably towards an adult who knows what the child is doing and why.

REPEAT, REPEAT AND REPEAT

This is a strategy that is commonly called 'broken record'. It is useful to use when you do not want to enter into any kind of dialogue with a child. For example, if a child has not complied with a reasonable request from you then you would repeat your request – 'I would like you to give Janet her pencil back.' Pause. 'I would like you to give Janet her pencil back.' It is important that if the child wants to debate the point you calmly repeat your request. In this technique non-compliance is absolutely unacceptable, so it is important that the 'broken record' is not repeated endlessly. There will have to be stated consequences and sanctions for non-compliance.

CIRCLES

To work well there has to be consistent use of these circle time techniques across the whole school and on a regular basis in the classroom. They will not work effectively if just you and one teacher are using them.

If a child is finding social situations difficult, or is not managing to work well within a small group of learners, then some kind of formal adult intervention could work. A small group of volunteers needs to be gathered together weekly to discuss how to support the child and how to help them with their difficulties.

This is a strategy that needs to be discussed with parents and has to have a specified time limit. Whilst it is taking place it needs teaching assistant and/or teacher involvement in the weekly meetings of the circle of friends.

Circle time is a technique that is used in many classrooms to raise self-esteem, solve social problems and discuss and prevent conflict. It is a complicated but extremely effective technique that needs specific ground rules that are taught to both adults and children.

GIVING INSTRUCTIONS WITHOUT USING THE WORD 'NO'

Some children respond negatively to the word 'no' and it provokes confrontations. It can be avoided by rephrasing instructions. Avoid saying such things as 'No, you can't go out to play yet because you haven't finished your work.' Instead, say 'When you have finished your work you can go out to play.' In this way you are setting the same conditions, issuing the same instructions and telling the child exactly the same thing within exactly the same ground rules without using the word 'no'.

CONSEQUENCES AND CHOICE

It is important to let children know that they can, and need to, make choices about their own behaviour and that what they choose can have positive or negative consequences. This technique can also give children more control over their actions. Instead of stating the consequences of not taking a particular course of action, let the child see the consequences and make the choice for themselves. For example, rather than saying 'If you don't finish your work I will keep you in at lunchtime', say 'If you choose not to finish your work now you are also choosing to stay in at lunchtime – it's up to you.'

DISTANCING THE PROBLEM

Sometimes it is useful to discuss a child's behaviour as if it is separate from the child. If a child is causing problems in the playground, for example, and is finding it difficult to join in games, they are likely to be unhappy and will find that other children don't want to play with them. Their behaviour needs to change before they can be accepted. Questions to the child that distance or externalise the problem in some way might make it easier to talk about and consequently easier to solve. For example, 'Not joining in games in the playground seems to be a problem that is making you unhappy. What do you think we can do to solve the problem and help you have a better time?'

Sometimes children can kick or hit, and it becomes a pattern of behaviour that they find difficult to stop and consequently they will become more and more unhappy because their peers will isolate them. This can be externalised and distanced by asking questions such as 'You seem to be getting into difficulties with your hands and feet today. What do you think you need to do to stop them behaving badly?'

ALLOWING A WAY OUT

If a child is behaving inappropriately, and this involves them not doing what is asked or refusing to follow instructions, they can often place themselves in a situation with no way out. This can lead to more frustration and more anger.

Adult intervention will be needed to give them a way out of the situation they have placed themselves in. This can include giving them a simple instruction and telling them that you will come back later to see how they are getting on. For example, 'I will come back in five minutes. Please make sure that you are sitting in your place and carrying on with [whatever task is appropriate].'

Giving the child choices also works well in this situation. You could say something like 'I would like you to sit down in your seat and carry on with [the task], or if you would rather come into the corridor with me we could do [suggest another task].'

USING THE RIGHT WORDS

Choosing an appropriate way of speaking to children can be extremely useful and can help in all kinds of classroom management situations. Here is a list of 'Dos and 'Don'ts' – effective and ineffective ways of speaking to children.

Effective ways of speaking will include using 'I' frequently. Instead of saying 'You should be working' or 'You shouldn't be doing that', say 'I need you to start writing now' or 'I need you to stop doing that'. This change of emphasis often removes the sense of being blamed that many children with low self-esteem can feel when they are challenged about their attitude or behaviour. Other examples of effective ways to speak to children include:

● 'I think what you did manage to finish was OK. It looked very interesting' or 'I liked the way you did that [include detail of what it is they did].'

● 'Look, I know you are feeling upset about this [name what it is if it helps], but the rule is that you [re-emphasise the rule].'

● 'You are not allowed to hurt other children. No-one is allowed to do that. They are not allowed to hurt you and you are not allowed to hurt them.'

● 'I can see you are upset. I'll give you some time to calm down. So sit here, settle down and we will talk about it in [set a time – no more than five minutes later].'

● 'Look, tomorrow is a new fresh day and we'll all start again' or 'Today's a new day. We'll all make a fresh start.'

Ineffective ways of speaking will rely on blaming, rather than showing understanding, and will draw upon simple but unhelpful statements of what is already obvious. This will include some or all of the following:

● 'Why can't you always be like this?', 'Why can't you do as you are told for once' or 'Why can't you start your work on time for once?'

● 'What's the matter with you – why do you always behave like this?' Variations include 'Why do you never do as you are told?', 'Why do I always have to tell you twice?'

● 'That's ridiculous behaviour – you're just being childish' or 'You're just overreacting.'

● 'I don't know what's wrong with you – of course it's not difficult.'

● 'Look, do I have to keep telling you the same thing over and over again' or 'How many times do I have to tell you.'

● 'You are not the only one I have to help you know' or 'You are not the only person in the group.'

MODELLING THE APPROPRIATE BEHAVIOUR

If we expect children to be calm, then all adults need to be calm. If we expect good manners and politeness, then we need to model this kind of behaviour so that there are consistent expectations for children. Some children have backgrounds and a home life that, unfortunately, models very inappropriate behaviour. This means that it is only when they are in school that they are shown how to behave to acceptable social norms.

ACTING OUT ATTITUDES AND BEHAVIOUR

This is a strategy that is only appropriate with an individual, or two children who have had some kind of conflict. Meet with the child, or pair of children, on their own and act out the inappropriate behaviour or attitude, saying 'This is how I saw you behaving.' Beware! If you do it really well it can look ridiculous and seem quite amusing to the child. When you have acted out the behaviour you need to have a discussion about how to prevent this kind of behaviour in future. The best way to use this tactic is to be brief and don't use it as an opportunity to reprimand or embarrass the child.

BEING POSITIVE

This is about praising behaviour, attitudes and work that you think is good in a positive way, bearing in mind that individual children will react to praise in different ways. It can also be about using positive language to prevent or resolve negative situations. However you choose to do it, it should be genuine, simple and specific. For example, 'I noticed that you are using your best handwriting, well done' or 'You have tried really hard to get that drawing just right. I'm very pleased.'

Sometimes it is effective to give public praise, but you have to know your children. Some children will prefer praise to be given in private or even by trying to distance it through a kind of third party. One of these techniques is to use such phrases as 'Mrs Rogers has been telling me that you behaved really well at lunchtime. I am very pleased.' Some children like being praised in a positive way by their peers and it can be useful in a small group if you ask children questions such as 'Peter, what has John done really well today?' or 'John, what do you think is really good about Peter's work?'

The main lessons to be learned from using some of the tactics that have been described is that all children need attention. As far as possible the attention that they are given should be given supportively, calmly, clearly, consistently and positively.

ACTION ROUTES FOR MANAGING INDIVIDUAL CHILDREN

Let's try and use some of the suggestions that have been made so far in this chapter in a practical way. It will be useful to plot how you would deal with an incident and stop the behaviour escalating and continuing.

If you are a teaching assistant, think of a classroom or playground incident where a child behaved inappropriately. If you are not already working in a school think of an incident with a child you know where there were problems with their inappropriate behaviour – don't be precious about this, it happens in all families.

When you have done this, try and follow the 'Action route' (photocopiable page 83) by reading the suggested action and then writing down what you would have done at each stage. Don't forget to think about all the suggestions and ideas that have been made in this chapter and earlier in the book when writing how you would deal with the incident. When you have finished the activity, think how you would modify it. It might be that you feel that there are too many stages, or that there aren't enough and that you would like to add one or more.

CONTROL TACTICS

So far this chapter has been concerned with developing a repertoire of useful skills and the assumption has been that managing children's behaviour involves skills that can be learned and developed. Many of these skills, once they have been learned, also need to be practiced. Many of them are short, simple and to many adults who work in school they are, or quickly become, second nature. Most of these quick control tactics can be used alone or in combination with others, and also alongside all kinds of suggestions that have already been made in this chapter.

NON-VERBAL CONTROL TACTICS
1. Using eye contact.
2. Raising the eyebrow during eye contact.
3. Frowning.
4. Giving a 'filthy look'.
5. Shaking your head whilst doing any combinations of tactics 1–4.
6. Pointing a finger, or other useful gesture, in combination with tactics 1–5.
7. Smiling – not with any of numbers 2–6.
8. Using a calming gesture with your hand at the same time as a smile.
9. Nodding at the same time as smiling.
10. Using a quiet gesture of finger on lips, on its own or with 1, 2, 3 or 8.

SOUND AS A CONTROL TACTIC

1. Clapping hands.
2. Tapping on the desk with a hard object.
3. Closing the door loudly.
4. Snapping fingers.
5. Saying someone's name.
6. Coughing.
7. Using words as signals, such as 'Right, is everyone ready?' at the same time as any combination of tactics 1–5.

CONTACT AS A CONTROL TACTIC

1. Moving to stand close to a particular child.
2. Moving to sit close to a particular child.
3. Walking towards a child purposefully.
4. Removing an object, such as a pencil, that is causing problems.

LOOKING IN CONTROL

When any of the control tactics are being used, whoever is using them needs to be in charge, or if you like *in control*. This needs to happen right from the start, every day and every time you are starting work with a new or different group. In other words, control tactics will only work effectively when the adult *is* in control of the situation, and then they need to be used straight away or as soon as it becomes necessary.

When children and adults meet for the first time, a great deal of information needs to be shared. In terms of children in groups or classes, there is a constant jockeying for position in terms of the social aspect of the group or class (who is friendly with who, who has fallen out, and so on). There is also the academic aspect of who is cleverer than who, or who can't do some of the work very well. If we agree that there are all kinds of 'beginnings' during a school day, then it is important that we get them right.

In *Managing Behaviour Problems* (Hodder & Stoughton), Diane Montgomery suggests that there are facial expressions that adults use which can influence how a group of children reacts (page 19). It is vital that your facial expression conveys confidence. A smile that signifies you are unsure or anxious will be picked up by children in a split second. A mirror can help with practising gestures, and saying aloud some of the verbal techniques will help your confidence grow when using them. As a teaching assistant, you will need to enter any 'teaching' situation with a firm tread, shoulders back and an easy confident pose.

CLASSROOM RULES

In this final section, let's make it very clear that every school and every classroom has to have rules. Ideally, there should be a consistent approach and there should be a high degree of commonality about what is allowed and what children must not do. Schools do vary in their ethos and in their approach to discipline, control and the management of groups and classes. This means that it is impossible to suggest an exemplar list of 'rules', other than that they should be as positive as possible and that they tackle the kind of behaviour and attitudes that are important. At the beginning of each year most effective classes will negotiate a set of 'golden' classroom rules that they will emphasise throughout the year. They might include variations of the following:

- Be thoughtful and polite.
- Be well mannered.
- Never hit anyone.
- Never call anyone names or tease them.
- Stay out of the classroom at break or lunchtime.
- Keep everything tidy.
- Always walk when moving around in the classroom.
- If you borrow something return it.
- Respect other people's property.
- Do your homework on time.
- Work quietly.
- Listen to the teacher.
- Put your hand up if you want to answer a question.
- If you want to leave the room, ask.

Once rules have been agreed, established and shared with children, all adults in the school and parents, they will need to be enforced. Children will not remember all the rules and will conveniently forget them. There is little point in setting up the rules at the beginning of the school year and then forgetting about them. There will need to be constant reminders, and both the teacher and you the teaching assistant will have to explain them carefully to individual children. There are various strategies for doing this. They include:

- Laying down the law: 'Put your hand up if you want to answer a question.'
- Giving an explanation: 'You must put your hand up so that we can all hear you and no one shouts out.'
- Expressing righteous indignation: 'I am really disappointed that so many children are still shouting out answers.'
- Generalising: 'I'd like to see a few more children putting their hands up today.'
- Being calmly specific: 'You know the rule. No one is allowed to shout out. You must put your hand up.'

- Asking general questions: 'Why is it important to put your hands up when you want to answer a question?'
- Asking a more specific question: 'Why do I tell you to put your hands up every time you want to answer a question?'
- Negotiating a rule: 'When we are answering questions some children are still not putting their hands up. How can we stop that happening?'
- Using faint praise (to someone who isn't quite obeying the rule, but is making a real effort): 'That's good John, you have managed to put your hand up three times today.'

Rules, if they are to work at all, are there to strike a balance between rewards and sanctions. It is important to stress the importance of rewards and the fact that they should far outweigh sanctions. It is also useful for both teachers and teaching assistants, and indeed the whole school, to make their rewards both 'external' and 'internal'.

External rewards are given to a child and have usually been earned by them. They are often visible, like a gold star, a prize in assembly, a comment in a book that is more significant than usual.

Internal rewards usually come from within and are the feelings of satisfaction when something has been done well. Praise, a smile, a word of encouragement, can often trigger a child's internal reward system. Remember, a smile and a nod of encouragement is easy to give and always good value.

CONCLUSION

This chapter has been about minimising the barriers some children erect that affect how they learn and whether they are able to reach their full potential. The two most difficult barriers to remove are those related to inappropriate or disruptive behaviour and a child's low self-esteem. As a teaching assistant you will have to work alongside such children, whether individually or in groups, to support them in the classroom, manage their behaviour and maximise their learning. There will have to be discussions with the class teacher to determine what support is necessary. There will also need to be collaboration with the class teacher about the amount of intervention that is necessary in terms of encouraging independence, modelling appropriate behaviour and using the necessary control tactics and reward/sanction systems with reluctant learners.

ACTION ROUTE

STAGE 1
This is when the inappropriate incident first happens.

ACTION TO BE TAKEN
Ignore the behaviour unless it is endangering another child or causing intense distress to someone else.

STAGE 2
You cannot ignore the behaviour, or if you have ignored it, you find that it has happened again.

ACTION TO BE TAKEN
Give an instruction or make a direct statement.
What exactly would you say? Some ideas could include repeating a rule or reminding the child of a rule.

STAGE 3
The steps you have already taken have not been totally effective and after a period of time the behaviour has happened again.

ACTION TO BE TAKEN
Repeat Stage 2 or give the child a clear choice. In other words, you are stating the consequences of what will happen if the behaviour continues.
How will you give the choice? What will the sanction be?

STAGE 4
The behaviour persists and you take final action.

ACTION TO BE TAKEN
You have already told the child what the consequences of their actions will be – now carry it out.
What are you going to do? How will you do it?

STAGE 5
The incident is over and you have dealt with the behaviour. There now has to be a return to 'normal' relationships.

ACTION TO BE TAKEN
You will have to speak to the child, discuss their behaviour and start again in terms of your relationship with them.
What will you say? Where will you discuss the behaviour with the child? Will you involve the class teacher?

the fullest picture possible of what is happening. Some of the activities that accompany this kind of visual vigilance can and should include:

LOOKING AHEAD

It is possible to look at a group of children and, because you know them, anticipate what they are likely to do and what might happen that could cause problems. Being vigilant enough to stop problems before they arise is a very effective skill, because it could well be the difference between a low-key approach of quietly speaking to a child and the need to resolve a very disruptive dispute that prevents teaching and learning taking place at all.

COMMENTING TO AN INDIVIDUAL

Occasionally it might be necessary to speak out loud to a child. This can have two important functions. It tells the child that you are aware of what they are doing and sends a signal to the rest of the class that they are being monitored.

CHECKING WORK IN PROGRESS

By visually sweeping the class or group of children, and by backing this up by 'patrolling' the classroom, you will be able to see what is happening in terms of who is, or who is not, working. You will also be able to note who is finding the work too difficult and who might be finding the work too easy.

STOPPING AND STARTING

If it is obvious that an individual or a group of children is having difficulties understanding or is just not willing to start the task that has been set, it may be necessary to stop the lesson and repeat instructions. Make sure that this time, when you tell everyone to start, you immediately go to the unwilling child or group, and help them to make a good start. It might also be useful to take an individual or small group to one side and help them quietly, so that everyone else does not have to stop what they are doing.

CONSTANT REMINDERS

It is very effective to show children that you are aware of everything that is happening by noticing behaviour that is outside the actual task that they are working on. For example, it is important to give reminders about sharing, about waiting their turn and about simple social behaviour such as the use of 'Please' and 'Thank you'. When noticing children who are being positive in these ways, it is good to praise them because it will show that you are noticing their good behaviour and will possibly help their self-esteem.

BEING IN CONTROL IN THE CLASSROOM

When any adult is 'teaching' and 'in control', they will have planned what they are going to do and say and they will, if they are effective 'teachers', have planned what the children are going to do. All this planning will be wasted unless they are in control of how the children react and behave when they are explaining and describing the objectives and tasks, and also when they are supervising, observing and supporting children during the tasks.

CONTROL SEQUENCES

Every teaching and learning group is a volatile maelstrom of personalities, attitudes and feelings, where individuals are working alone for their own gains as well as in groups where co-operation and perseverance may be needed. In *Classroom Teaching Skills* (Houghton Mifflin), Ted Wragg suggests that 'control' of both children and the curriculum is extremely important and key to effective teaching and learning. The following examples are clear and simple strategies that can be learned and developed by teaching assistants. Once they become a natural part of teaching skills they can be used quickly and easily.

When you look at each of the five control sequences (photocopiable pages 103–108) try performing them as you would in front of a group or class of children. Use a mirror and don't be embarrassed. Practice makes perfect.

The spaces on the control sequences are there for you to note down any good ideas about how you would personalise each sequence, in terms of what it is you would do or say that you feel would work for you and, if you are working in school, would also work for the children in the classes you support. In the case of the 'move closer' part of the sequence, try and describe how you would do it by using descriptive words, such as *purposefully* or *vigorously*. It may be worth looking back at some of your favourite behaviour management strategies from Chapter 4, as you will be able to use them as part of the control sequences.

HELPING CHILDREN UNDERSTAND

It is very important for adults in the classroom to be able to focus on children's learning and how they can help each child learn more efficiently. One way of doing this as a teaching assistant is to improve your *explanations*, that is how you explain to children what they need to do, why they need to do something, how they can achieve the best results and when they need to complete a specified task. An *explanation* could be part of a control sequence (see photocopiable pages 103–108). For example, if you are explaining how to do something to a child who is reluctant to start a piece of work, you could use your voice and body in an appropriate way by choosing the right words, gesticulating, moving round the room and maintaining eye contact to enhance your explanation.

I have identified at least seven different types of explanations, set out below, that will be used in most, if not all, classrooms over a period of time. Some are easier to use than others and some will be more useful for different ages of children. But, whatever age and whatever ability the children you support, you have to be able to explain clearly and concisely so that they can understand.

CLASSROOM PROCEDURES

These could include explanations regarding rules and routines, or they could be about procedures in specific subjects. For example, in literacy it will be necessary to explain the pattern of each lesson or remind children what they need to do when they are sitting on the carpet.

FIVE

CONVERSATIONS IN THE CLASSROOM

Before looking at questions and answers in more detail, let's look briefly at how people talk to each other – how adults talk to adults, how adults talk to children, how children talk to adults and how children talk to each other are all extremely important.

Eric Berne in *Games People Play: The Psychology of Human Relationships* (Penguin) created a term known as 'Transactional Analysis'. He suggested that when two people communicate, they do so in three basic styles:

1. As a parent *[P]* where they tell, assert, dominate, criticise, offer advice and discipline.
2. As an adult *[A]* where they behave in a logical, rational way, which involves working towards the solution to a problem as well as reasoning, listening and suggesting.
3. As a child *[C]* where the main response is to feelings. It can be an enthusiastic way of communicating, full of fun, but it can also be angry and rebellious. Dealing with these feelings can be challenging.

Conversations in the classroom can be an important part of each child's learning process. Transactional Analysis can begin to help us analyse successful and less successful ways of both holding and benefiting from these important dialogues. Obviously, there are many different versions and variations, but looking at the following examples should help you recognise some of the problems and pitfalls that can occur during conversations with children as well as making you aware of the need to think carefully about the style of conversation you use and how effective it is as a communication tool.

When you have looked at each example it will be useful to think of similar conversations you have had in the classroom and how effective these were with children at communicating what you had intended to say.

PATTERNS OF CONVERSATION USING TRANSACTIONAL ANALYSIS

SAME STYLES

EXAMPLE
Adult: 'How many of these questions have you managed to answer?'
Child: 'I'm doing really well. I've just finished the fifth one.'

DIFFERENT STYLES

EXAMPLE
Adult: 'What are you doing? You can't just go around sticking your pencil in other children like that.'
Child: 'It was their fault. [Shouting] And why are you always picking on me?'

CROSSED STYLES WHERE RESPONSE IS AN UNEXPECTED STYLE

EXAMPLE
Adult: 'This is very good, I am very pleased with what you have done.'
Child: 'No it's not. It's rubbish and I haven't finished it yet.'

DELIBERATE CROSSED STYLES

EXAMPLE
Child: 'I can't draw this sketch map at all. It's really a waste of time and I don't think I can be bothered to finish it.'
Adult: 'Let me see how I can help you.'

Example: 'What is the difference between a mammal and a reptile?'
Correct answers would include comparison of the two species, such as 'Warm blooded/cold blooded' or 'Feed own young/don't feed own young.'

OPEN-ENDED QUESTIONS THAT EXPLORE IDEAS
This applies to areas of knowledge with few set answers. It encourages reasoning and interpreting. It is useful when resolving playground disputes, but can also be used effectively in the classroom.
Example: 'How do you think John felt when you did that?' or 'How would Jamal feel if you stopped being friends with him?'

OPEN-ENDED QUESTIONS THAT ENCOURAGE COMPARING INFORMATION AND IDEAS
These are usually used when focusing on different sources of information.
Example: 'When you look at the evidence do you think this metal called brass will attract the magnet or not?'

OPEN-ENDED QUESTIONS TO ENCOURAGE EVALUATION AND DECISION-MAKING
These are very difficult to word correctly for younger children and are probably best left for a very able group of older children.
Example: 'Would it be fair to say that… '

CLASSROOM MANAGEMENT SKILLS
This final chapter is reviewing some useful classroom management skills that can and must be used alongside some of the other skills that have been suggested in previous chapters. In Chapter 1 there was a 'Self-appraisal questionnaire' (pages 19-20) that identified some of the general and broad roles that, if they don't already exist, will soon be part of every teaching assistant's job. It is useful to repeat a similar activity here, but this time asking questions that are related to specific skills and techniques on classroom management, and to ask for some evidence that the technique is being used.

SELF-ASSESSMENT OF CLASSROOM MANAGEMENT SKILLS

Read each of the skills or techniques on the 'Self-assessment of classroom management skills' form (photocopiable pages 109-110) and then write down one of the following numbers alongside each statement:

1 if you think you are good at using this skill or technique
2 if you think you are OK but need to practise or learn more
3 if you think you are either not good at using this skill or technique, or would like to use it but need to learn more.

In the space beneath each skill or technique give yourself some feedback. Consider, for example, how you use the technique, what you do or say, when you use it, whether it works or is useful.

When you have completed the form, share your responses with your class teacher. They might be able to help you become better in those areas where you have written 2 or 3. The whole activity could also be used in your performance management review. For example, those areas where you have entered 2 or 3 could be used in target setting for the next performance management cycle.

RELATIONSHIPS AND ATMOSPHERE

If you have responded in a largely positive way to the 'Self-assessment of classroom management skills', then you will be well aware of the need to develop a relationship with children that creates a working atmosphere which provides excellent opportunities for each child to learn.

There are five basic principles which, if used consistently, should help you create a positive atmosphere and better adult–child and child–child relationships in the school.

1. LET THE CHILDREN KNOW THAT YOU VALUE THEM

We all need to see ourselves as worthwhile and able to succeed. It is an essential part of raising self-esteem. Children need to be treated with respect, valued as individuals and encouraged to work to their potential.

2. PROVIDE WORK THAT IS RELEVANT TO THE CHILDREN

The National Curriculum and national testing will dictate much of what has to be taught, but working alongside teachers will enable you to interpret this content to produce interesting, creative and relevant experiences for the children. If teachers and teaching assistants work as a team, it is possible to know each child's interests and their strengths and their weaknesses. By observing, listening and discussing the teaching and learning that takes place you will know what kinds of activities stimulate the children and help them learn more fully and effectively.

- hot tempered
- out of control
- violent.

Passive words include:
- timid
- meek
- put upon
- lacking confidence
- mild
- complaisant.

The one missing is 'quiet'. This is a difficult behaviour to place or categorise. It may be interesting for you to consider where you think it should be placed.

To be assertive is to be more successful than if you behave in a timid or aggressive way, and by being assertive you are outlining the following rights:
- I have the right to be heard and taken seriously.
- I have the right to set priorities within my own areas of responsibilities.
- I have the right to express feelings and opinions.
- I have the right to say No.
- I have the right to make mistakes at times when I am trying my best.

LEARNING TO BE ASSERTIVE

If you are not a naturally assertive person, and yet you recognise its importance in your role as a teaching assistant, it is possible to learn how to behave in this way. By being assertive in difficult circumstances it is possible to improve your feelings about yourself, give yourself confidence and prevent yourself from feeling powerless and out of control. The following step-by-step guide to assertion suggests the kind of script that you can learn which applies to relationships you will have with children, colleagues and parents.

STEP-BY-STEP GUIDE TO ASSERTION

To create the guide the following scenario has been developed:

> You have had to speak firmly to a child who has been persistently calling other children names. He suddenly starts shouting at you and saying that he hates you.

Read each step of the guide below. It is quite long and you may want to change some of the words to suit how you would speak, or it may be possible to shorten each step in some way. If you do, it is important not to lessen the meaning or the impact.

1. SUMMARISE THE BEHAVIOUR THAT CREATED THE PROBLEM

Do this simply, straightforwardly and unemotionally, remembering to use 'I' as often as possible. For example, 'I don't like it when you call other children names and I certainly will not allow anyone to shout at me.'

2. STATE EXACTLY HOW YOU FEEL, NOT HOW ANYONE ELSE FEELS

For example, 'I am very concerned that you have been name calling and I'm sad, upset, and angry with you that you have shouted at me in that bad tempered way.'

3. DESCRIBE CLEARLY AND SIMPLY WHY YOU FEEL LIKE THIS

For example, 'First of all, you know that you are expected to be friendly with everyone and I feel concerned, because name calling and teasing is not being friendly. Secondly, shouting at an adult makes me feel extremely unhappy because you know that this is something very serious and you have broken a school rule.'

4. SYMPATHISE OR EMPATHISE WITH THE CHILD'S POINT OF VIEW

For example, 'I can understand that you find some of your friends irritating and I am sure that I make you cross sometimes.'

5. SPECIFY EXACTLY WHAT YOU WANT THE CHILD TO DO

You should also say what you would be willing to do to find a solution, a compromise or a way out of the situation. For example, 'I want you to calm down immediately and stop shouting. I want you to promise me that you will stop calling other children names. If you have a problem with some of your friends, you must tell me and I will try to help you.'

6. DECIDE WHAT YOUR RESPONSE WILL BE

It is important that whatever you decide should clarify the position and not threaten the other person. For example, 'If you calm down immediately you will be able to carry on playing in the playground, and I will talk to you again later when you are less bad tempered.'

FIVE

BEHAVIOUR STYLE

There have already been two examples of self-assessment in this book, which have offered opportunities for you to discover more about certain styles of professional behaviour and how you use them as a teaching assistant. The 'Behaviour-style self assessment' form, below, identifies six aspects of adult behaviour in school. Looking at and developing classroom behaviour in ways that promotes an ethos that encourages high standards of teaching and learning is extremely important. It is not just how children behave that influences standards, but also how teachers and teaching assistants relate to each other and to children.

The six aspects of adult behaviour in school that we are concerned with, some of which you will recognise, are as follows.

Giving help to children: This relates to how you work with children who either need extra help or are off task for some reason.
Spoken behaviour: How you use your voice with children.
Non-verbal behaviour: This is concerned with how you use your body as part of your 'teaching' style.
Eye contact: This is how you actually look at children, and can apply to when you are praising them or admonishing them for any reason.
Reaction to disruption and conflict: This relates to the time spent dealing with inappropriate behaviour or attitudes.
Control style: This includes some of the ways problems are dealt with.

BEHAVIOUR-STYLE SELF ASSESSMENT

To complete this final self-assessment you need to be prepared to watch yourself working honestly and truthfully. Choose a specific time of day where there is a 40-minute slot when you will be doing something that you do regularly.

Read through the 'Behaviour-style self-assessment' form (photocopiable pages 111–112) beforehand so that you are familiar with it. Complete it as soon

as possible after the 40 minutes has ended. The 'Length of time' column on the form is for you to say approximately how long you spent doing this particular activity. The 'Comments' column should be completed in terms of 'When I did this was it a positive thing to do and did it help the children?' or 'Was it a negative experience in the sense that it didn't help the children?'. The 'Giving help to children' section asks you to differentiate between boys and girls. It is important to think carefully about whether you treat boys and girls in similar ways. They can certainly behave and learn very differently, but both need consistent approaches that maximise learning opportunities for them. Certain ways of speaking and delivering the teaching will influence the learning and behaviour as appropriate.

SUMMARY OF SKILLS FOR TEACHING ASSISTANTS

It is important to look through your responses to all the self-assessments in this book, including the one that you have just completed, to check that what you do most of the time as a teaching assistant helps children learn more effectively by boosting their self-esteem and treating them with respect. If children grow in self-respect and self-knowledge, they will be able to grow into adults who can respond to others with the same kind of respect and understanding. All the strategies suggested in this book have taken into account the impact of teaching assistant behaviour on children's self-esteem and self-confidence. At the same time all the strategies have also recognised that each child needs praise for what is hard work, genuine achievements and progress.

Here is a final list of attributes that teaching assistants should possess. It is not a definitive list – although it is my idea of the most important attributes a teaching assistant should possess. The attributes could easily be modified and prioritised, but if all teaching assistants could use these skills and build on them, schools would be better places and children would become more skilful learners. I hope you will recognise yourself in the list as well as being able to see that many of the suggested attributes have been part of the discussions throughout the book and can be learned and developed as essential 'teaching' skills.

- Giving praise and encouragement for achievement and progress.
- Giving praise for behaviour that has been asked for.
- Using clear and simple age-appropriate language to describe tasks.
- Breaking down activities into manageable chunks.
- Having the ability to repeat instructions to make sure that they are clearly understood.
- Differentiating tasks to match individual or small group needs.
- Changing and altering activities and tasks to meet children's needs.
- Modelling the behaviour that is required and the attitudes to work that are needed.
- Supporting children in their work with a view to developing their independence.
- Speaking, questioning and explaining, using language that children can understand.
- Securing the child's/children's attention before starting to speak, explain or ask questions.

● Using firm and friendly control strategies.
● Being able to discuss work and behaviour with children firmly, sympathetically but assertively.
● Ask a variety of closed and open-ended questions.
● Listen to children and respond appropriately to their contributions.

CONCLUSION

I have tried to make it clear that teaching assistants have a key role to play in both the provision of high quality education to children and in the smooth running of schools. They have a multiplicity of roles which will change, if not regularly, then over a period of time. This will mean that teaching assistants will have to be flexible and able to meet new challenges, rather than imagine that the job they are doing today will remain the same tomorrow and forever.

To do this, of course, will mean taking up staff development opportunities and being an enthusiastic and willing participant in performance management. The development of personal skills and strategies that will not only promote learning, but will also help manage behaviour and deal with such issues as conflict, bullying, racism and discrimination, will have to involve a professional and reflective approach that will help you as a teaching assistant work closely and effectively in a professional team This is not easy, but is essential if teaching assistants are going to be leading figures in helping teachers to create, maintain and develop a positive and supportive learning environment in the classroom.

In fact, the final conclusion to draw is that teaching assistants should probably be likened to 'superman' or 'superwoman'. They need good communication skills with children and the wide range of adults who work in and who visit schools. They need to have the ability to respond to both children's emotional, behavioural and intellectual needs and, at the same time, to manage busy, ever changing and extremely diverse workloads. Is this you? I expect it is. If, in addition, you have motivation, tact, professionalism, sensitivity and a good sense of humour and are able to manage change effectively, then there are many, many schools near to where you live who either already have, or need, your experience and expertise.

CONTROL SEQUENCE 1

This is usually a starting point – literally the first sequence to use when an individual or group is not on task or is behaving inappropriately. For example, by not starting work or talking rather than concentrating on the task in hand.

Signal of action ⎯⎯⎯⎯⎯⎯⟶ Move closer ⎯⎯⎯⎯⎯⎯⟶ Take action

SIGNAL OF ACTION
This will be one of your usual signals, such as a cough, a look, a raised eyebrow or a glare.

MOVE CLOSER
This is the obvious follow up and in fact can take place at the same time as your 'signal of action'.

TAKE ACTION
You are trying to stop something you don't like from happening, and at the same time making sure that what you want to take place starts happening. If your 'signal of action' and 'move closer' haven't changed the behaviour then you need to say or do something that is simple and appropriate. For example, 'Stop fiddling with your pencil please and start your work' or 'Write the date quickly and then start the first question.'

SIGNAL OF ACTION

MOVE CLOSER

TAKE ACTION

SELF-ASSESSMENT OF CLASSROOM MANAGEMENT SKILLS – CONTINUED

THE TRANSITIONS BETWEEN ACTIVITIES IN THE CLASSROOM

● I am able to make sure that the transitions between activities are relatively smooth, and free from excessive noise. ☐

● I plan any activity changes so that they don't just happen and I know when the activities are supposed to stop and start. ☐

THE BEHAVIOUR AND RESPONSE OF THE CHILDREN

● I am aware of everything that is happening in my group. ☐

● I am able to make sure that each child is aware that I am watching them and that I know exactly what they are doing. ☐

● I am able to move around and give signals to all the children about their work and behaviour. ☐

● I have positive rules and rewards related to the school and class rules. ☐

ENDING ACTIVITIES

● I make sure my activities end properly and tidily, without noise or confusion. ☐

● I try to introduce some forward planning by suggesting what will be happening the next time I work with the individual or group. ☐

MY ATTITUDE

● I have an appropriate attitude towards the children – neither too severe nor too permissive. ☐

● I am approachable in the classroom and in the playground. ☐

BEHAVIOUR-STYLE SELF-ASSESSMENT

GIVING HELP TO CHILDREN	Length of time	Comments
To boys		
To girls		

SPOKEN BEHAVIOUR	Length of time	Comments
Firm, decisive, confident voice		
Lacking in confidence, unclear and mumbling		
Loud, shouting		
Speaking too quickly		
Speaking monotonously		
Voice too harsh		

NON-VERBAL BEHAVIOUR	Length of time	Comments
Confident stance		
Confident smile		
Assertive use of body		
Walking round the room		
Standing in front of the class or group		
Frowning		
Standing close		
Using signals, such as pointing, fingers on lips		

CONTINUED...

BEHAVIOUR-STYLE SELF-ASSESSMENT - CONTINUED

EYE CONTACT	Length of time	Comments
Eyes darting here and there		
Clear and direct to individual or class		
Used with raised eyebrows		
Glaring at children		
Frowning at children		
Direct eye contact with gestures, such as pointing, smiling		

SPOKEN BEHAVIOUR	Length of time	Comments
Handling it so that disruption stops		
Handling it so that disruption continues		

CONTROL STYLE	Length of time	Comments
Trying to ignore disruption		
Moving close to disruptive child and staying until disruption is over		
Giving a direct instruction		
Using humour to defuse a situation		
Making an assertive statement		
Sending a child away from the group or out of the room		
Reminding children of the rules		
Displaying anger		

Based on material © Warwickshire LEA